MUSTANG
1964¹⁄₂–1973

Mike Mueller

CRESTLINE

This edition published in 2013 by
CRESTLINE
A division of BOOK SALES, INC.
276 Fifth Avenue Suite 206
New York, New York 10001
USA

This edition published by arrangement with
Motorbooks International.

First published in 2000 by MBI Publishing
Company, 400 First Avenue North, Suite
400, Minneapolis, Minnesota, 55401

Library of Congress Cataloging-in
Publication Data

Mueller, Mike, 1959–
  Mustang 1964 1/2–1973 / Mike Mueller.
     p. cm.
  ISBN: 978-0-7858-2972-0
  1. Mustang automobile—History—20th
century. I. Title.
  TL215.M8M843 2008
  629.222'2—dc22

2008009202

On the front cover:
The big-block-powered GT 500 joined the
GT 350 in 1967. Those driving lamps in the
grille were mounted either close together or
at opposite ends, depending on state laws
where they were sold. Some local laws
prohibited the in-tandem mounting shown
here. *Tom Glatch*

On the frontispiece:
Mustangs didn't come any bigger or badder
than the Boss 429, offered in limited numbers in 1969 and 1970. Beneath that huge
functional hood scoop is the
375-horse "Shotgun" big-block with aluminum "semihemi" heads.

On the title page:
The GT package introduced in April 1965
featured the Interior Decor Group. Included
was simulated wood grain paneling for the
dashboard, a sporty five-dial instrument
cluster in place of the dull Falcon instrumentation, a simulated walnut steering
wheel, bright pedal trim, and pistol-grip
door handles.

On the back cover:
Nothing could stop the Mustang after it
hit the ground running in April 1964. Two
models were initially offered, a classy
coupe and an always-sexy convertible. A
third body style, the sleek 2+2 fastback,
appeared later in September. Since that
time, the galloping horse has symbolized
the true essence of the term "pony car."

Edited by Steve Hendrickson
Designed by Dan Perry

Printed in China

CONTENTS

ACKNOWLEDGMENTS　　　　　　　　　　　　　　**6**

INTRODUCTION
TELLING THE PONY TALE　　　　　　　　　　　　**8**

CHAPTER 1
HORSE BREEDING, FORD STYLE
Development and Design　　　　　　　　　　　　**17**

CHAPTER 2
SETTING THE WORLD AFIRE
April 1964: the Mustang Debuts　　　　　　　　**27**

CHAPTER 3
HAPPY TRAILS?
Mustang Ups and Downs, 1965–1973　　　　　**47**

CHAPTER 4
PUTTING THE SPURS TO THE PONY
GT Mustangs, 1965–1969　　　　　　　　　　**69**

CHAPTER 5
VARIATIONS ON THE THEME
Carroll Shelby's GT 350 and GT 500　　　　　**85**

CHAPTER 6
SNAKE BITE
Big-block Cobra Jets, 1968–1971　　　　　**109**

CHAPTER 7
AT THE SPEED OF SOUND
Mach 1 Mustangs, 1969–1973　　　　　　　**127**

CHAPTER 8
LARGE AND IN CHARGE
Boss Mustangs, 1969–1971　　　　　　　　**139**

CHAPTER 9
EPILOGUE
Celebrating the Rest of the Pony Car Story　　**157**

INDEX　　　　　　　　　　　　　　　　　**168**

ACKNOWLEDGMENTS

Birthdays never have meant much to my family, except for my brother, Dave Mueller. He has surprised this not-so-humble author more than once, including on my twentieth birthday in May 1979. I was in college and my trusty 1967 Ford Galaxie was on its last legs. I didn't have two pennies to rub together, nor did I have any bright prospects as far as replacing my daily transport was concerned. What did he do? He put a bow on his beloved 1967 Mustang coupe and gave it to me as a present.

I then proceeded to drive his once-proud horse into the ground in only a few years, but it's the thought that counts, right? I thought that particular gift represented one of the greatest things anyone has ever done for me. Not only did the 1967 coupe get me around for a few years, it also helped foster my interest in both Mustangs and cars in general. That interest then blossomed into a career. So there you go, Dave. I basically owe everything to you.

The check's in the mail.

Additional thanks for helping me melt down yet another deadline go to my sister and her husband—Frank and Kathy Young in Champaign, Illinois—for putting up with me during so many photo junkets through the Midwest. My old buddie Ray Quinlan, also of Champaign, once again deserves kudos for helping me locate photo subjects, as does another great friend, Bill Tower, of Plant City, Florida. And who can forget (I know I can't) Donald Farr, my former boss at Dobbs Publishing (now a part of Petersen Publishing) in Lakeland, Florida. For some strange reason Donald has always been there when I need him—it will be impossible to ever pay him back for his patience and generosity. I am certainly not worthy.

The same goes for all the wonderful people who responded to my demands for photographic and research support. Two comrades, Steve "The Housewife" Statham in Austin, Texas, and Tom Glatch in Brookfield, Wisconsin, again came to the rescue with some wonderful Mustang photos—in focus, to boot. Historical black-and-white material came from the hardest working gal in Detroit, Paula Lewis, and her partner, Dan Erickson, both of Ford's Graphic Arts & Photomedia Services in Dearborn. Another old boss, Jonathan Stein at *Automobile*

Quarterly, allowed me access to *AQ*'s collection of Ford press release photos, which were scoured through by trusty Stuart Wells—Stuart, you are indeed the man. Historian and longtime friend Robert Ackerson in Schenevus, New York, also opened up his archives for the umpteenth time—Bob, we really must meet some day. Two other great sources, literature dealer Walter Miller in Syracuse, New York, and advertisement dealer George Reed in Selinsgrove, Pennsylvania, graciously supplied me with brochures, ads, and such.

There were so many other helping hands out there, including various property owners who so willingly allowed me to photograph a Mustang or two on their land. I can't name you all, but I will not forget. Nor can I overlook the guys at Floyd Garrett's musclecar museum in Sevierville, Tennessee, including Floyd himself. Floyd's righthand man, Jason Thompson, and his able assistant, Will Kenny, evaporated more than a gallon or two of sweat while helping me photograph Jackie Jones' rare 1971 Cobra Jet coupe. Another notable name is Jay Murray of the Georgia Regional Mustang Club here in Kennesaw, Georgia. Jay helped locate a photographable Mustang or two at the last minute.

Then there are the men and women behind all the Mustangs (and a few rivals) that make appearances on these pages. In general order of appearance, they are: 1964-1/2 convertible (blue), Sam Munro, Dunedin, Florida; 1967 GTA convertible, Ed Werder, Plantation, Florida; 1967 Plymouth Barracuda Formula S, Mike and Betty Gansen, Greene, Iowa; 1970 Plymouth Hemi 'Cuda, Jim Ludera, Bradenton, Florida; 1964-1/2 convertible (red), Robert Deale III, Marietta, Georgia; 1964-1/2 coupe, Dale Richeson, Tuscola, Illinois; 1964-1/2 Hi-Po convertible, Jim and Lynda Fannin, Bloomington, Illinois; 1965 coupe (black), Rod Batiste, Atlanta, Georgia; 1965 2+2 (blue), David and Marilyn Gass, Rantoul, Illinois; 1967 GTA fastback, Bernie and Zona Gail Doty, Strasburg, Illinois; 1968 coupe (light green), Tom Alexander, Humble, Texas; 1969 Super Cobra Jet convertible, Milton Robson, Gainesville, Georgia; 1971 Cobra Jet Mach 1, Charlie and Pam Plylar, Kissimmee, Florida; 1972 Olympic Sprint convertible, Ralph Gissal, Land O Lakes, Florida; 1973 convertible (gold), Tom and Carol Podemski, South Bend, Indiana; 1967 T-5 convertible, Johnnie and Rachel Garner, Rock Hill, South Carolina; 1965 A/FX drag car, Dave Geiger, Elkhart, Indiana; 1967 Chevrolet Z/28 Camaros (pair), Paul McGuire, Melbourne, Florida; 1969 Pontiac Trans Am, Don Walden, Tarpon Springs, Florida; 1974 Pontiac 455 Super Duty Trans Am, Paul Markey, Pinellas Park, Florida; 1966 Hi-Po GT coupe (yellow), Jim and Lynda Fannin, Bloomington, Illinois; 1965 GT convertible (red), Frank Chalker, Kennesaw, Georgia; 1967 GTA convertible (blue), Max and Joyce Dilley, Urbana, Illinois; 1969 GT convertible, Scott and Ginger Boss, Wimberly, Texas; 1965 Shelby GT 350, Mike Bell, Houston, Texas; 1965 Shelby GT 350R, Harris Conner, Chamblee, Georgia; 1966 Shelby GT 350, Tom and Ruthi O'Brien, Tuscola, Florida; 1966 Shelby GT 350H, Jim and Lynda Fannin, Bloomington, Illinois; 1967 Shelby GT 500 (white), Bob Mahoncy, Elm Grove, Wisconsin; 1968 Shelby GT 500KR convertible, Curtis Burton, Houston, Texas; 1969 Shelby GT 350 (dark green), Dennis and Kate Crow, Oakwood, Illinois; 1969 Shelby de Mexico GT 350 coupe, Steve Ooley, Carmel, Indiana; 1970 GT 500 fastback, Bill and Barbara Jacobsen, Silver Dollar Classic Cars, Odessa, Florida; 1967 Shelby GT 500 "Super Snake," David Loebenberg, St. Petersburg, Florida; 1968-1/2 428 Cobra Jet fastback (white), Dick Spain, Decatur, Illinois; 1968-1/2 428 CJ convertible, Gregg Cly, Mustang Muscle and More, Garland, Texas; 1971 429 Cobra Jet coupe (white), Jackie Jones, Young Harris, Georgia; 1969 Cobra Jet Mach 1 (red), Dennis and Kate Crow, Oakwood, Illinois; 1970 Mach 1, Walker Ford, Clearwater, Florida; 1971 Mach 1 (red), Nathaniel Key, Jr., Lithonia, Georgia; 1970 Boss 302, Bernia and Zona Gail Doty, Strasburg, Illinois; 1969 Boss 429 (red), Brett Cooper, Marietta, Georgia; 1970 Boss 429 (blue), Barry Larkins, Daytona Beach, Florida; 1971 Boss 351, Gregg Cly, Mustang Muscle and More, Garland, Texas; 1979 Indy Pace Car replicas (pair), Karl and Betty Zrnich, Brooksville, Florida.

I will never be able to thank each and every one of you enough for your kind cooperation.

—*Mike Mueller*

TELLING THE PONY TALE

The more things change, the more they don't always stay the same. Take new car introductions for example. They're nowhere near as exciting as they once were, and probably never will be again. Remember those larger-than-life banners? The balloons and confetti? Those mysterious plain brown wrappers? The teasers and the mounting hype? Doesn't anyone care anymore? Frankly, no. These days there are just too many marques, too many models, too many sales pitches. And too little that is novel or unique. One car is as good as the next, and you can't tell a Buick from a Toyota.

To make the American people stand up and take notice, a new model would have to be revolutionary. It would have to capture hearts on the first glance. It would need to generate the sort of irrational appeal that causes hundreds of thousands of people to rush dealerships, checkbooks in hand, demanding the object of their obsession. To create an overnight sensation today,

a manufacturer would have to offer drivers something they had never seen before—like a car with the spirit of a wild horse.

No one had seen anything like the four-wheeled sensation that hit the ground galloping on April 17, 1964. This wasn't merely a new model, it was an entirely new breed of automobile. It had a long hood and a short rear deck. It had buckets seats and a floor shifter. It was both sporty *and* practical, fun *and* affordable. It was loved by both young *and* old. It was Ford's Mustang—in *Car and Driver*'s words, "easily the best thing to come out of Detroit since the 1932 V-8 Model B roadster."

No new car before, not even ol' Henry's first flathead, had ever caused such a ruckus. None since has rocked our world with such force. When Dearborn introduced America to the pony car it not only made news, it made history. Ford's publicity push was unprecedented in scope, as was the media's response. The car made headlines well beyond the automotive press. Lee Iacocca and his baby even scored concurrent covers on both *Time* and *Newsweek*.

Equally unprecedented was America's response. Not-so-tall tales of police protection at dealerships and people sleeping overnight in the Mustang they intended to buy abounded in the spring of 1964. Wide-eyed gawkers of all ages, not just potential buyers, also gathered wherever a Mustang set its hooves. Feeding frenzies on dealer lots and traffic snarls on Mainstreet USA were commonplace. By the time the dust had settled, Ford had broken Detroit's record for a brand-new model's first-year sales—a record it had established with the all-new Falcon just four years before.

Dearborn's sales estimate for the Mustang's first year—100,000—went by the wayside after only four months. Nearly 419,000 found buyers by April 1965. Ford sold its 1 millionth Mustang in March 1966, then the 2 millionth followed in 1968. More

Dearborn's first pony car wasn't the only thing to hit the starting line going full bore. Ford's marketing campaign for the Mustang was unprecedented in both size and scope.

the unexpected...

Ford Mustang Convertible

M·2587

A PRODUCT OF
Ford
MOTOR COMPANY

Mustang hits
the starting line
full bore!

Here's Ford's new kind of car . . . and no car ever hit the road quite so ready for action. Mustang has a long, long list of goodies now, not six months or a year after introduction. Let's check down the list:
1. Three V-8's, from the supersmooth 164-hp version with hydraulic lifters through a strong 210-hp two-barrel, right up to the solid lifter-header exhaust high-performance 271-hp stormer. And that's not the end; the whole Cobra kit bolt-on array is available. (You want the four-Weber 343-

horse wild one? Just let us know.)
2. Transmissions? The V-8 choice starts with the all-synchro 3-speed manual. Or four-on-the-floor. Or Cruise-O-Matic Drive. All with floor shifts.
3. What else? A special handling package (included with high-performance V-8's) that makes the Mustang solid as a Pullman car on the corners. A Rally Pac that combines tach and clock with sweep-second hand. And, just to show we're versatile, air conditioning, a six-cylinder saver, power steering

and all the other *dolce vita* items.
We hope we're not immodest, but the Mustang four-seater starts life with the kind of equipment and options most cars take years to come by. And the kind of rock-solid handling. And the toughness and durability it takes to build a going competition machine.
Come down to your Ford Dealer's and take a long, careful look. If we've skipped anything that would make your heart glad we'd like to hear about it—but what could it be?

For a positively detailed, authentic scale model of the new Ford Mustang, send $1.00 to Ford Offer, Department CB-1, P.O. Box 35, Troy, Michigan. (Offer ends July 31, 1964.)

TRY TOTAL PERFORMANCE
FOR A CHANGE!

FORD
Mustang · Falcon · Fairlane · Ford · Thunderbird

than 35 years after its much-ballyhooed birth, America's original pony car was still rolling strong as ever in the year 2000, with total sales of some 7 million cars.

That's not to say that there weren't weak moments during those three-and-a-half decades. Most notable in most Mustangers' minds were the Mustang II years of 1973 to 1978. While bad feelings have softened toward those weak-kneed, downsized models in recent times, the classic Mustang clubbers' case remains closed: Ford more or less stopped making "real" Mustangs after

1973. An even-tighter-clenched contingent feels the cutoff should be 1970. And there are still diehard purists—descendants of those who cried when the T-bird grew two more seats, perhaps—who won't look at any Mustang built after 1966.

Varying opinions aside, the Mustang's first generation did run from 1964 to 1973. Although the body got bigger and overall weight grew, the basic platform carried on beneath the skin. And the image on the outside remained the same: lively, youth-oriented, fun yet functional.

Ford's Mustang is still rolling strong more than 35 years after its earthshaking introduction in April 1964. The present generation first appeared in 1994, just in time to mark the model's 30th anniversary. Appearing here with a classic 1964-1/2 convertible is a 1994 GT droptop.

Which Came First, Horse or Fish?

No one can forget what the Mustang meant to the marketplace when it exploded onto the scene on April 17, 1964. With its sporty appeal, youth-conscious affordability, and lightweight, compact stance, Iacocca's baby instantly defined an entirely new breed of American automobile. It also set sales records, and changed the manner in which American automobiles were sold.

Few American automobiles stand as tall in the nostalgic limelight as the Mustang. It has come to be known as the first, and the definitive, pony car. But what most fans of the Mustang don't realize is that Chrysler Corporation actually beat Ford to the punch in this new market. More than two weeks before the Mustang was released to an eager marketplace, Plymouth's sporty, compact Barracuda debuted on April 1. It was all but lost in the Mustang frenzy.

Like the Mustang, the Barracuda was an affordable compact dressed up with sporty imagery. Included in the $2,365 base price (with a six-cylinder; the 273-ci, two-barrel V-8 upped the standard price to $2,496) were front bucket seats, a bucket-style rear seat that folded down, and simulated knock-off wheel covers. But unlike the Mustang, the Barracuda did not feature a totally fresh look. Its long-hood, short-deck "fastback" profile was the result of a little hocus-pocus supplied by stylist Dave Cummins. He used the largest expanse of glass ever installed on an American car to mask another plain fact: The Barracuda was simply a gussied-up Valiant—as plain a car as they came in the early 1960s—with an enormous, eye-catching rear window tacked on. As for the name, apparently no one at Plymouth knew that, in the slang of the early 1960s, a "barracuda" was a very loose woman, loose enough perhaps to turn pro.

Although totally overshadowed by its wildly popular rival, Plymouth's Barracuda was no flop. Humble sales reports showed

Ford gets credit for originating the pony car breed, even though Plymouth actually rolled out its Barracuda first. A rocket scientist isn't required to explain the situation. The Mustang was an overnight sensation, while the Barracuda was just a Valiant dressed up with a huge glass fastback. *Chrysler Historical Collection*

23,443 models hit the streets in 1964. Another 60,168 followed in 1965. Plymouth officials had to be happy with those numbers. Critics, on the other hand, weren't so gay. As the sports-minded editors of *Car Life* saw it early in 1964, the Barracuda "needs some development if it is to match with performance the promise of its racy good looks. As it is right now, it's just a novel little hardtop that won't swim away from anything."

Things began to change in 1965 when Chrysler engineer Scott Harvey, a rally driver during his free time, put together the Formula S performance package. Along with some truly sporty suspension upgrades, the Formula S option also included a muscled-up 273 V-8, a four-barrel-fed small block that now pumped out 235 warmly welcomed horses. According to *Car and Driver*, the 235-horse 273 transformed the second-edition Barracuda

"from a flabby boulevardier into a rugged middleweight."

Heavyweight status arrived in 1967 as the Barracuda, like the Mustang, was fitted with its first big block—Chrysler's 383-ci V-8. This 280-horsepower powerplant had to be shoehorned into the 1967 Barracuda's engine bay, even after designer Milt Antonick had restyled and reshaped Plymouth's pony car platform with an eye toward making more room for more engine up front. Antonick's sweet body was also offered in two forms, a sexy fastback and a polite "notchback" coupe.

Chrysler's high-winding 340-ci V-8 appeared in 1968 to help create a better-balanced Barracuda. A wonderful combination of big-block muscle and small-block sprightliness, the 275-horsepower 340 dropped in with room to spare—optional air conditioning could be added; it couldn't fit on an early 383 Barracuda, nor could

A sexy new body and big-block power enhanced the Barracuda's appeal in 1967. The top model that year, at least from a horsepower perspective, was the Formula S fitted with the 383-cube V-8.

brakes and steering. The 'Cuda reached its performance zenith in 1970 and 1971 as both the 440 Six Barrel and 426 Hemi V-8s became options. Big-block options were then dropped after 1971 as the musclecar era wound down. Dwindling sales forced the cancellation of the Barracuda itself, as well as the Challenger, three years later.

Mustangs, meanwhile, continued rolling on, albeit through those dreaded Mustang II years. Two other long-running rivals, General Motors' F-bodies Chevrolet Camaro and Pontiac Firebird, are still around too, but apparently not for long. The Mustang may soon be the last of the breed left standing. As for the first of the family, Ford might not have technically earned that honor. Nonetheless, they don't call 'em "predatorfishcars." Be the name 'Cuda, Camaro, Firebird, or Javelin, they're still all known as "pony cars."

power brakes. Pounds were spared as well, meaning the 340 Formula S Barracuda could run circles around its nose-heavy big-block big brother. Most (maybe even all) Mustangs in 1968 were also no match for this commonly overlooked muscle machine as far as all-around performance was concerned.

Plymouth's pony car performance image became impossible to overlook after Cliff Voss' Advanced Styling Studio totally redesigned the Barracuda for 1970. Chrysler's all-new E-body platform, which also supported Dodge's slightly larger Challenger, was designed not only to look like a million bucks, but also to house Chrysler's largest V-8s without sacrificing preferred accessories like air conditioning and power

The performance zenith for Plymouth's pony car came in 1970 with the introduction of the Hemi 'Cuda. Beneath that big "Shaker" hood scoop were 425 real horses that made this fish one of the fastest musclecars of the day.

Less certainly wasn't more in the Mustang's case. First generation models grew in size for both 1967 and 1971. Shown here is a 1967 GTA convertible—the "A" was a one-year-only designation for automatic-equipped GTs.

The same certainly couldn't be said for the second-generation models that followed after 1973. A true compact, the Mustang II may have sold like hotcakes early on in the economy-conscious 1970s, but it never captured the imagination of the masses the way its predecessor did a decade before. It also lost its appeal not long after it took *Motor Trend*'s Car of the Year honors in 1974. Once Americans got used to the fact that gasoline had turned to gold, they apparently no longer felt they had to compromise their standards any further. Fortunately Ford restarted the Mustang legacy in 1979 with a more comfortable, better performing machine, and the "modern" pony car hasn't looked back since.

Yet as successful as the Mustang still is today, nothing Ford's best minds can ever do will spur the car on to anywhere near the great heights gained during those heady days back in the 1960s. Nor does Ford expect such results—600,000 cars a year is an outrageous sales performance standard akin to Cy Young's record 511 career wins. That no pitcher will ever approach Young's lofty total is not so much a matter of depreciating talent as it is an indication of how much major league baseball has changed in 100 years. Much the same can be said for the new car game. Today's market is so much more fragmented than it was 30-something years ago; the pie was sliced into fewer pieces then, and it was easier to be a standout.

If you can't join 'em, beat 'em. Ford planners were initially inspired by Chevrolet's Corvair Monza, a sporty compact with bucket seats. But instead of simply following Chevy's lead, Ford did the Bow-Tie boys one better. Squared off here against the Corvair in March 1962 is one of the many early concept creations that laid the groundwork for the Mustang's development. *Ford Motor, Company photo courtesy of* Automobile Quarterly

Purists who cried foul when their polite pony put on weight in 1967 had another thing coming four years later. The closest thing to Lee Iacocca's original idea available during the years 1971–1973 was a scale model.

Ford established a record for first-year sales when it introduced the compact Falcon in 1960. Lee Iacocca (right) then dashed that record five years later with the first Mustang. With the Falcon is Iacocca's right-hand man, Donald Frey. *Ford Motor Company*

Mustang meant many different things to many different drivers, but most witnesses recognized the sporty aspects of the pony car breed. Ford officials didn't mind promoting these aspects at any competition venue available, including the Bonneville Salt Flats. In September 1968, they sent three specially prepared Mach 1s to Utah, where the cars established 295 speed and endurance records. *Ford Motor Company, photo courtesy of Automobile Quarterly*

As much as Iacocca has always wanted the world to think of him as the greatest automotive marketing genius of all time, great timing was the real key to the Mustang's instant success. Iacocca was simply smart enough to recognize the opportunity when it presented itself. He could also count: 1946 plus 16 equals 1962. As *Motor Trend*'s Jim Brokaw later wrote in 1971, "Iacocca knew what sold cars to young people in those days and he knew, as did anyone who bothered to note birth statistics from 1946 on, who was shortly going to engulf the market, a veritable army of young, aggressive customers." Experts in the late 1950s were predicting that the 15- to 29-year-old age group would grow by as much as 40 percent during the 1960s thanks to the influx of the baby boomer set.

Iacocca rose to the vice president's chair at Ford in November 1960, then almost immediately began working to take advantage of the wave of boomers then poised to become legal motor vehicle operators. Thus

began the project that would eventually evolve into the Mustang. Iacocca of course didn't work alone on that project. Names commonly lost in Lee's giant shadow included, among others, product planning manager Donald Frey, who followed his superior up Dearborn's corporate ladder; Frey's special projects assistant Hal Sperlich; and Donald Peterson, who became Ford Motor Company president in 1980. Joe Oros, working under Gene Bordinat, was the prime mover as far as styling was concerned. Designer Gail Halderman also made major contributions.

Many people deserved portions of the credit that Iacocca was so willing to collect all by himself. When later asked why the top man got all the attention in 1964, Frey had one quick answer: "He was my boss." Peterson was graciously magnanimous in 1989 when asked where the credit really was due: "Don Frey said, 'We gotta have something sporty.' Lee Iacocca sponsored the effort all the way. Harold Sperlich put the program together. Joe Oros styled a beauty. Henry Ford

II said, 'Now you're talking.' And from the very beginning, the Mustang has been a giant success."

Even if he claimed all of it, Iacocca deserved much of the credit. "He had a major role in marketing, creating the whole mystique and the advertising campaign," added Frey. "And he said to make [the Mustang] a four-seater, which was a key product decision. Up until that point, we had been thinking two-seaters. But he was right; there was a much bigger market for a four-seater." And if there was any one contribution that was key to the entire project, it was Iacocca's ability to pry loose the company purse strings to fund the thing. "He took something like five shots with the senior officers of the company to convince them to put money into the car," said Frey.

Ford took a gamble, bucking the trends of the day to introduce a radical new design. The other players in Detroit were convinced the revolution would be crushed in the marketplace, but it was they who were crushed by the Mustang stampede.

HORSE BREEDING, FORD STYLE

Development and Design

Pony car roots can be traced back to 1955, the year Ford wowed Americans with another long-hood/short-deck wonder. Like the Mustang, the Thunderbird was an instant hit that Dearborn simply couldn't build fast enough to suit crazed customers. Even so, the cute little two-seater's limited scope doomed it even before it was introduced. Who cared that initial sales ran well beyond predictions? Dearborn's braintrust concluded that there was little or no future in selling 15,000 to 20,000 personal luxury convertibles a year. The word came down from the top to redesign the lovely classic as a four-place model a few weeks before the T-bird's September 1954 debut. The bigger, roomier "Squarebird" then arrived, with a backseat, in 1958. Purists' cries of foul were quickly drowned out that year by the proverbial cash register's "cha-ching" as Thunderbird sales nearly doubled.

Yet as much as the 1958 Thunderbird apparently struck down the principle that less is more, Ford planners in the late-1950s still

kept their minds open to the possibilities of marketing another diminutive automobile. They had eyes; they could see the growing wave of foreign compacts landing on American shores.

When Ford took a second shot at the small car thing, it did so with the affordable, economical Falcon, introduced for 1960 along with two rivals, Chevrolet's Corvair and Plymouth's Valiant. Despite mundane styling and modest performance, the simple, budget-conscious Falcon struck a chord with buyers. Ford's first Falcon outsold Chevrolet's rear-engined compact by nearly a 2 to 1 margin on the way to shattering Detroit's record for instant success. First-year sales for Dearborn's new compact totaled 417,174.

Such unprecedented prosperity right out of the blocks was certainly nothing to sneeze at. Yet there were some around Ford who wondered if the results could have been even greater had the Falcon not been such a plain-Jane. Among this group was the man who had just been promoted to Ford Division's top office—

Above: Various two-seat sportster ideas were drawn up in Ford styling studios in the early 1960s. Shown here is a September 1961 proposal for a Falcon-based sports car. *Ford Motor Company, photo courtesy of* Automobile Quarterly

Left: Many heart-broken T-bird lovers were waiting for Ford to reintroduce a sporty two-seater in the early 1960s, and designers even played with various concepts built for two. Then along came the Mustang I in 1962. Sports car lovers rejoiced, but it was only a promotional tease. *Ford Motor Company*

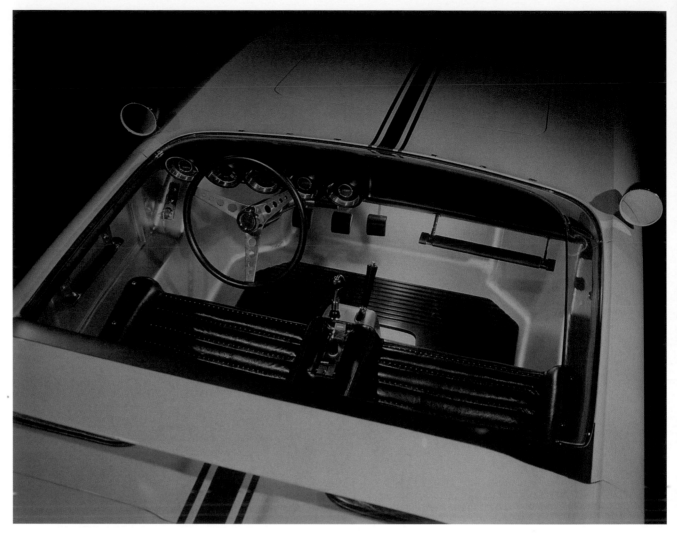

The Mustang I's interior was race-car Spartan, which was only right since the car was not created for regular-production consideration. It was purely a test-track queen and a show circuit star. *Ford Motor Company*

the 36-year-old former marketing manager, Lee Iacocca. Unlike his conservative predecessor, Robert McNamara, Iacocca was hot for something hot.

Ford's efforts to stay competitive had led to a new-found interest in performance, something the company had all but given up on in 1957. That year McNamara had agreed to the infamous Automobile Manufacturers Association "ban" on both factory-supported racing and the general promotion of high performance. General Motors, meanwhile, kept racing—at the track and on the street. After two years of watching rivals run away in Detroit's horsepower race, Ford engineers finally began toying with go-fast goodies again in 1960. Ford's renewed interest in performance, or at least sports appeal, suited Iacocca's vision perfectly.

Immediately after his promotion in November 1960, Iacocca assembled a group of creative minds. Included were product planners Donald Frey, Hal Sperlich, and Donald Peterson; marketing man Bob Eggert; public relations manager Walt Murphy; and racing guru Jacque Passino. This group met every week for 14 weeks at Dearborn's Fairlane Motel and thus became known as the "Fairlane Committee." The Total Performance campaign, through which Ford sought to boost its image by returning to the racetrack, came out of these meetings—with Passino running the show.

The main focus, though, was the little car that would eventually become the Mustang. Various ideas for this vehicle were quickly formulated, but the best inspiration probably came from outside the group. "It started with a few guys sitting around," remembered Frey. "We started watching registrations of the Corvair, which was a dog. I guess in desperation they put bucket seats in the thing, called it the Monza, and it started to sell. We got the idea that there must be something to it. And that's how it all started—watching Monzas."

When all the initial brain-storming was through, the basic parameters for Ford's response to the Corvair Monza involved a similar sporty image based on a body that, like the original Thunderbird, featured a long hood and short rear deck. This small fun machine would be no longer than 180 inches and would weigh in at about 2,500 pounds. And, it was hoped, it would cost no more than a dollar a pound. Last, by the boss's specific demand, it would have room for four. Iacocca wasn't about to repeat the mistake made in 1955. Two seats alone did not a sporty car make, and he would prove this at all costs. The group began putting ideas down on paper in earnest in late 1961.

Earlier that summer, Gene Bordinat's Advanced Styling studio had produced various conceptual drawings of sporty two-seaters, as more than one mind at

Ford was still considering something along the lines of a lighter, lower-priced 1955 T-bird. Iacocca himself even gave Bordinat the go-ahead for a full-fledged prototype project that would eventually mislead the ascot-wearing crowd into believing Ford was preparing to introduce an honest-to-goodness sports car—an agile little performer with no top and no back seat.

Early in 1962, Bordinat made Bob Maguire and Damon Woods chief stylists of this project, with Maguire overseeing the exterior, Woods the interior. Under them were executive stylists John Najjar and Jim Sipple, and it was their team that drew up plans for an amazing midengined sports car. Racer Dan Gurney took one look at the Najjar/Sipple team's work and gave an enthusiastic thumbs-up. Then along came engineering vice-president Herb Misch, who was in

Ford Styling chief Gene Bordinat (middle) was an early supporter of the two-seat sports car plan. To his right is Herb Misch, engineering vice president. Seated in the low-slung Mustang I is Roy Lunn, chassis engineer and the main man behind the car's birth.

search of a special concept car to knock 'em dead during the 1963 new model introductions to be held later that fall. Bordinat offered him the midship two-seater, and he accepted.

Transforming clay into sheet metal began in May 1962. Chassis engineer Roy Lunn—who later designed Ford's world-beating race car, the GT-40, and also headed up Kar Kraft, home to the Boss 429 Mustang— was charged with creating the mechanical beauty beneath the aluminum skin. A tubular-steel "birdcage" space frame complete with roll bar was welded up as a home for a midship-mounted V-4 engine and four-speed transaxle, which were borrowed from Ford of

Germany's Taunus front-wheel-drive compact. Control arms at the corners were also tubular steel and were suspended by coil-over shocks. Wheels were cast magnesium measuring 13 by 5 inches.

The European 1,500-cc V-4 was boosted from its standard 89 horsepower to 109 by increasing compression to 11:1 and adding a lumpier cam and dual Weber carbs on a special intake. The clutch was hydraulic and the shifter worked via cables. Brakes were discs up front, drums in back. Inside, both the steering wheel and foot-pedal assembly could be adjusted to fit the driver, this because the leather-covered aluminum bucket seats were fixed in place.

Dimensions were 90 inches for the wheelbase, 154 inches for overall length. It was a mere 28.8 inches tall at the cowl (39.4 inches at the top of the roll bar), and it weighed only 1,544 pounds. As for its name, that came courtesy of John Najjar, who was especially fond of a certain legendary World War II fighter airplane. Built by North American Aviation, that plane was the P-51 Mustang.

Ford's first Mustang was completed by October 2, 1962, just in time to be shipped to its public unveiling at Watkins Glen, New York, where it had everyone talking. *Car and Driver* called it "the first true sports car to come out of Dearborn." Barrie Gill of the *London Daily Herald* claimed it was "one of the most exciting cars I have ever ridden in."

On the track at Watkins Glen that day, Dan Gurney reportedly drove the two-seat midengined Mustang to 120 miles per hour. The rumor mill then began churning even faster. In its December 1963 issue, *Motor Trend* announced that "Ford will produce a sports car to compete with the Corvette." Of course, Iacocca, Frey, and the rest knew differently. The first Mustang was nothing more than a publicity stunt, and a damned good one at that. The idea behind it was to prime the pump, to familiarize the Mustang name with the public, and to associate that name with something definitely sporty. Iacocca was then more than happy to hear the American public clamoring for a Mustang of

its own, even if the car it would eventually receive was an entirely different animal.

Development of that new breed was well under way early in 1962. Up to that point, the only thing Iacocca had seen that came close to his four-place ideal was Bordinat's "Allegro," an intriguing concept but not exactly what the boss was looking for. He then decided to kick off a design competition with three players involved: the Advanced, the Ford, and the Lincoln-Mercury design studios. Six mockups were presented to division management in August 1962, and according to Iacocca, the initial favorite was a Ford studio design named "Stiletto." Projected costs for the Stiletto were prohibitively high, however, and it was killed then and there.

That left the design that Bordinat claimed was the head-and-shoulders choice among the group. Called

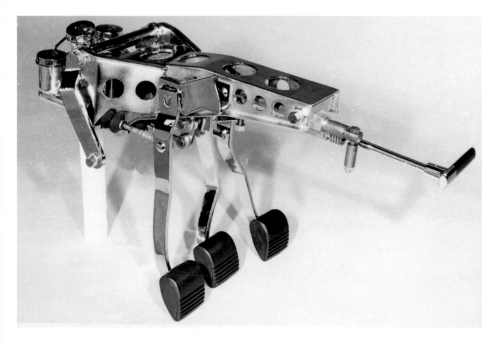

The Mustang I was powered by a four-cylinder engine originally created for the stillborn Cardinal, a front-wheel-drive compact that was initially planned for the world market in 1962. After Ford killed the Cardinal here in America, it was transformed into the Taunus 12/15 M, which was built in Germany and sold in Europe from 1962 to 1970. The 1,500-cc Taunus engine produced 109 horsepower in Mustang I trim. *Ford Motor Company, photo courtesy of* Automobile Quarterly

Among the Mustang I's many unique features was its adjustable foot pedal assembly. The bucket seats were fixed, so the pedals could be moved to match the driver's reach. *Ford Motor Company, photo courtesy of* Automobile Quarterly

"Cougar," this mockup was the work of Dave Ash, Joe Oros' assistant in the Ford studio. Oros had left Ash in charge during the competition because he had to leave town. The assistant then created the winning design, and history has since given his boss the bulk of the credit. Go figure. Ash can at least take solace in the fact that his design carried through with only minor changes right into production. Few styling nails have ever been hit so directly on the head so early in a design process.

The same, of course, couldn't be said for Ash's choice of names, one of many to appear on mockups during the development process. Before Cougar there was simply the project code "T-5." Some prototypes were simply considered "special Falcons," while others were adorned with the "Torino" nameplate. Oros preferred Cougar, and he accordingly campaigned for it with great vigor. Henry Ford II reportedly tossed "T-Bird II" about, but no one around Dearborn cared to catch it. In the end, the one name that fit like a glove ended up being the natural choice. Mustang it was.

But the Mustang couldn't come to life until Henry Ford II's office gave the final go-ahead. Iacocca approached the ivory tower on September 10, 1962, with an armload of cost studies and projections, knowing that his bosses would be leery of another new car project so soon after the Edsel fiasco of 1958–1960. He also knew they would question the viability of investing good money trying to satisfy the unknown demands of the baby-boomer wave, especially when the company was already set to spend some $250 million to retool the Ford Division line for 1965. Ford Motor Company President Arjay Miller was concerned about the bite this "youth car" would take out of Falcon sales.

Fortunately, Henry Ford II liked the idea, and his was the decision that mattered. Iacocca came away from what he called the toughest selling job of his career with an approval and a meager $40 million to develop and

tool up the Mustang. He eventually spent $65 million. He also only had 18 months to meet a March 9, 1964, deadline for "Job One," that being the first production example to roll off the Dearborn assembly line. Car companies typically allow about three years between approval and production start-up for a new model project. After the hard sell with Henry II's men, Iacocca probably thought, "Peanuts!"

Engineers had a head start on the project because the plan was to adapt as much of the Falcon's existing platform as possible. Suspension and steering components

were modified Falcon parts, as was the basic unit-body substructure—that is, the floor pan and cowl. Dimensions differed here and there with the most noticeable change involving the Mustang's height. The new car's Falcon-based floor pan was dropped down around the engine/trans to bring both the passengers and the roof closer to the ground. Cowl height in turn was cut. All this lowering was just what the doctor ordered to impart the sporty image Iacocca wanted.

The Mustang's "borrowed" heritage, on the other hand, also inspired more than a few slaps from critics

One year after the Mustang I debuted at Watkins Glen, Ford returned to the fabled racetrack with another show-stopper, the Mustang II—shown here at the 1964 Detroit Auto Show. *Oliver Young*

9-19-63
S-6679-4

The Mustang II began life as a stock-bodied preproduction car. A lowered roofline and modified nose and tail treatments were added, but remaining lines predicted the car that was to come in April 1964. *Ford Motor Company courtesy of Automobile Quarterly*

and jealous rivals alike. GM design chief Bill Mitchell called the final product "a Hamtramck Falcon"—an off-color crack referring to the Detroit suburb of Hamtramck, whose population was predominantly Polish. History too has since commonly referred to the original Mustang as a Falcon beneath the skin, but that description is too strong. "The Mustang had a lot of Falcon parts in it," said Gail Halderman, "but it was not a glorified Falcon as many believe."

The Mustang that inspired Bill Mitchell's "Pollack joke" was in fact a showcar built in 1963 to make one last publicity push before the final product debuted. After drawing so much attention with the midengine

Mustang two-seater at Watkins Glen in 1962, Gene Bordinat decided to return to the venerated New York track with a second "idea car" the following year. The plan was to provide a link between the two-seat sports car and the actual Mustang scheduled to arrive in 1964. Bordinat's ploy also involved a little trickery borrowed from his GM counterparts, who more than once before had taken a preproduction example of an unreleased new model and customized it into a showcar. It then looked like the new car evolved from the showcar, when, in fact, the reverse was true.

Bordinat's idea car was basically a standard Mustang with customized nose and tail treatments and a

While the car itself came together quickly in 1962, the name was another matter. "Cougar" was one of many considered, as demonstrated by the grille emblem shown here in May 1963. *Ford Motor Company courtesy of Automobile Quarterly*

The project code "T-5" was also considered, but was dropped, leaving "Mustang" to carry on alone. Ford then brought the T-5 badge back for pony cars exported to Europe, where the Mustang name was already a corporate-owned trademark.

lowered roof. Like Roy Lunn's two-seater, it too was painted white with blue racing stripes. It was named Mustang II as the first Watkins Glen show-stopper became Mustang I. At "The Glen" in October 1963, Iacocca told the press that showing off the Mustang II allowed Ford "a pre-test of likely customer responses to styling and mechanical innovations we may be considering for future production models."

Of course, by then the deal was all but done. Responses didn't matter, not even negative ones. *Motor Trend*'s psychics couldn't believe their eyes. In their words, the "Mustang II may herald the general lines of that division's upcoming sports car, but it likely isn't an actual prototype. It resembles the original Mustang not at all. It's rather a shame that the Mustang name had to be diluted this way."

Some six months later, Lee Iacocca would prove that *Motor Trend*'s critics were all wet.

SETTING THE WORLD AFIRE

April 1964: the Mustang Debuts

Outsiders got their first look at the Mustang in the fall of 1963 when Ford invited some of the nation's more prominent magazine journalists to Dearborn for a confidential briefing on what the public would see some six months later. All the top titles were represented, including *Time* and *Newsweek*, *LIFE* and *Look*, *Esquire* and *Sports Illustrated*. Their staffs were treated to a long day's worth of slide shows and speeches. But this was just the beginning. What followed in the months to come was the most extensive, most effective public relations push ever pulled off in the automotive industry.

Ford flooded the media, sending Mustang press kits to about 11,000 newspapers and magazines. Foreign-language versions were even shipped overseas. Ford dealers in 13 major markets were given their own presentations, and about 200 of radio's best-known disc jockeys were invited to Dearborn for firsthand test drives just weeks before the April 17 unveiling.

The official press introduction came Monday, April 13, at the New York World's Fair. More than 125 representatives from all forms of media showed up from the United States, Canada, and Puerto Rico. After listening to Iacocca speak about the youth-oriented market, the crowd was introduced up close and personal to the most anticipated automobile since Henry Ford replaced the Model T with the Model A in 1928. Later that day, the throng then set out in a caravan of Mustangs on a 750-mile rally run from New York to Detroit. This drive not only served to impress the press, it also allowed innocent bystanders along the way to get their first look.

An unprecedented broadcast barrage began on Thursday evening, April 16, as Mustang television commercials ran on all three networks at the same time. Countless print ads followed in

Above: Among the few complaints made concerning the new Mustang in 1964 was its plain Falcon-based dashboard.

Left: Nothing could stop the Mustang after it hit the ground running in April 1964. Two models were initially offered, a classy coupe and an always-sexy convertible. A third body style, the sleek 2+2 fastback, appeared later in September. The 1964-1/2 convertible shown here is one of 28,833 topless Mustangs built before "actual" 1965 production began in August 1964.

Production of 1964-1/2 coupes was 92,705. This coupe's finish, Pagoda Green, was one of five colors offered only on 1964-1/2 Mustangs. It is also powered by the 260-ci V-8, which was replaced by a 289 V-8 for 1965.

essentially every major magazine and newspaper beginning that weekend. But who had time to pick up a paper? Starting on Friday, much of America was busy flocking into the nearest Ford showroom to at least see the little car that was creating such a stir.

Buying one was not so easy. The few Mustangs on hand were immediately snapped up, and another 22,000 orders were placed that first day. A two-month wait for delivery was common, leading some potential buyers to extreme action to secure a showroom model right away. In Garland, Texas, 15 customers wanted a

local dealer's last Mustang. His solution was to give the car to the highest bidder, who then insisted on spending the night in it to ensure it wouldn't be sold out from under him before his check could clear the next day.

Other believe-it-or-not tales included dealerships locking their doors and calling the police when the rush grew too great. Reportedly a dealer in Pittsburgh put a Mustang up on a wash rack, then couldn't get it back down because of all the gawkers standing in the way. By some estimates, as many as 4 million people pushed their way into Ford dealerships that weekend alone.

Mustang buyers at first could choose from two optional Windsor small-block V-8s, the 260-2V (two-barrel) and 289-4V (four-barrel). The latter, shown here, was rated at 210 horsepower. A 200-horse 289-2V replaced the 260 for the 1965 model run.

Among the various running changes that set 1964-1/2 Mustangs apart from their 1965 successors involved the hood's front corners, which were beveled on early cars (left). The same area on 1965 Mustangs featured a sharp edge (right).

The corresponding edge on the "louvered" panel located to each side of the grille also was beveled for 1964-1/2 models (left). Again compare it to the sharpened edge on the 1965 panel (far right).

Opposite: Differentiating a 1965 model from a 1964-1/2 is essentially impossible at a glance. This black coupe, one of 374,346 built for 1965, is fitted with the attractive styled-steel wheel option, priced at $119.

Availability continued to be a problem beyond that first week as supply simply couldn't keep up with demand. The only real complaints heard by Ford concerning the new Mustang involved the difficulties finding one to buy. One famous telegram sent directly to Henry Ford II said it best:

> Henry Ford, I do declare
> You have your Grandpa Henry's flair
> He put a Ford in every home.
> You put a Mustang there.
> Congratulations.
> The wait out here is somewhat sickly;
> Could you fix me up more quickly?

Original company forecasts projected less than 100,000 Mustangs would be sold the first year, but Iacocca knew better. From early on his goal was to break the Falcon's record for new model first-year sales, and the battle cry around Dearborn in 1964 thus became "417 by 4-17"—the plan was to sell more than 417,000 Mustangs by 4-17-65. The tally on April 17, 1965, read 418,812— 1,638 more Mustangs in 1965 than Falcons in 1960.

Of that record-breaking total, 121,538 were so-called "1964-1/2" Mustangs. Introduced as it was smack in the middle of a model year, the first Mustang experienced an extended 18-month run that ended, as it should have, in August 1965. To keep things simple, most sources identified Ford's original pony car as a "1965" model. But various running changes did differentiate the cars built before August 1964 from those built afterwards, thus making it relatively easy to group the Mustang's first production run into 1964-1/2 and true 1965 categories. The most readily recognizable clue is that 1964-1/2 Mustangs used generators; 1965s used alternators. Production for the "true" 12-month 1965 model run was 559,451 Mustangs.

Midway through the 1966 run the Mustang broke yet another sales record held by the Falcon. Just before noon on Wednesday, February 23, the 1 millionth Mustang rolled off the Dearborn assembly line, making Iacocca's baby the quickest to reach seven digits. Interestingly, the tale of the millionth Mustang became intertwined with that of "Job One," the very first Mustang built in March 1964.

Massive Marketing

Two new kinds of cars debuted in 1964, one from Ford, the other from Pontiac. The latter, the GTO, introduced America to the musclecar. It also demonstrated just how massive a marketing campaign could be. Cooperative promotions included, among many other things, Thom McAn's GTO shoes and Max Factor's GTO cologne. One-hit wonders Ronny and the Daytonas released the song "G.T.O.," their lyrical tribute to the car that started it all for young speed freaks. Hurst Products, in cahoots with Petersen Publishing, even gave away the "GeeTO Tiger," a customized 1965 GTO, to a 19-year-old contest winner in the Milwaukee area.

The other totally new 1964 automobile, the Mustang, proved that "sporty" and "practical" could apply to the same vehicle. So too could "affordable." That last merit might have been enough of an enticement on its own for eager buyers, but Dearborn officials covered all bases with some saturation marketing of their own.

The blitz began on April 16, 1964, with an unprecedented domination of television commercial time during the coveted 9:30 to 10:00 P.M. time slot on all three networks. According to conservative estimates, the new Mustang made its way into 29 million American households on that Thursday evening. This was followed by a print ad push over the following week that included full-page advertisements in at least 24 national magazines and more than 2,500 major newspapers. Feature stories soon appeared in magazines of all kinds, from

Business Week to *Sports Illustrated*, *LIFE* to *Look*, *Popular Science* to *Playboy*. And let's not forget the coinciding cover stories in *Time* and *Newsweek*. Of Iacocca's mass-market marvel, the latter reported that "Ford is spending more than $10 million to imbed it in the national consciousness like a gumdrop in a four-year-old's cheek."

A seemingly endless stream of other companies was also more than willing to help spread the word. The Mustang name was borrowed by retailers selling everything from earrings to key chains, sunglasses to boots, hats to cufflinks.

Young people's clothes were especially targeted; one chain even named its youth department the Mustang Shop. The term *Mustang Generation* was born in California to describe the young, single set, and a *Wall Street Journal* front-page headline then used it atop a report on advertising targeted at the 20 to 34 age group.

Ford's merry marketeers didn't feel their targeting should stop at 20-year-olds. Or licensed drivers, for that matter. Predicting that children would soon be growing into young adults, Ford also became heavily involved in the toy business. The first 50,000 customers who responded to Ford's Order Holding Program in 1964 not only got a shot at the real thing, they also received a 1/25-scale plastic Mustang model supplied by AMT. Ford dealers stocked a 1/12-scale battery-powered Mustang supplied by the Cox company—or perhaps the older kids would have preferred a Philco-Ford transistor radio hidden in another 1/25-scale Mustang replica. Many other Mustang toys and models were produced and sold through a wide variety of aftermarket sources, including Matchbox, TomyToys, and Shredded Wheat breakfast cereal.

Above: Highly valued collector's items today, the AMF Mustang pedal cars were just children's toys in 1965. The American Machine and Foundry Company manufactured more than 118,000 Mustang pedal cars in various forms before ceasing production in 1972.

Right: Easily the most coveted Mustang pedal car is the Indy 500 pacer. Reportedly 100 of these were distributed to Indianapolis 500 Festival Committee members in May 1964. Less than a handful are known today.

Ford dealers reportedly sold about 93,000 Mustang pedal cars during the 1964 and 1965 Christmas seasons, before letting AMF take it on its own from there. The little $12.95 toys rolled on a 23-inch wheelbase and stood a scant 14 inches high.

But easily the best remembered approach to the truly youthful market involved the Mustang pedal cars, introduced just in time for Christmas 1964. Supplied by the American Machine and Foundry Company (AMF) of Olney, Illinois, and sold through Ford dealers, the "Midget Mustang" debuted late in 1964 to almost as much fanfare as its full-sized counterpart. A one-page *LIFE* magazine ad was one of at least a half-dozen major magazine advertisements inducing Mustang-minded parents to put their child behind the wheel of a pedal-powered pony car on Christmas morning.

The idea was first presented in prototype form to Lee Iacocca by AMF's Patrick Wilkins early in 1964. Iacocca liked the idea and production quickly followed. Priced at $12.95, the Midget Mustang's metal body measured a mere 39 inches from front to rear. It rolled on a 23-inch wheelbase and was only 14 inches high. Standard features included whitewall rubber tires with deluxe wheel covers, a steel, three-spoke steering wheel, a Rally-Pac instrument cluster decal, and a

working three-speed stick on the right-hand doorsill. Virtually all Ford-marketed Midget Mustangs were red, although rumors claim a few may have been painted light blue/gray. Of course it was also not uncommon to find Junior's pedal car repainted to match Dad's daily driver.

Yet another variation was created especially for the Indianapolis 500 Festival Committee. One hundred Indy Pace Car pedal cars were reportedly distributed to committee members. These mini-Mustangs were painted white with a blue stripe down the hood and deck lid. They of course also wore "Official Indianapolis 500 Pace Car" decals, and a hand-lettered serial number tag was added beneath the skin. Only four legitimate Mustang Pace Car pedal cars are known today—one of which brought $1,700 at auction in the 1990s.

Ford dealers sold some 93,000 Midget Mustangs from December 1964 through the 1965 Christmas season. Dearborn chose to drop the promotion in 1966, but AMF officials weren't deterred and continued producing Mustang pedal cars and marketing them themselves.

AMF had to remove the "Ford" lettering in 1966. It also added new spinner hubcaps and an updated grille like that of the real thing. Other changes included GT-style racing side stripes in 1967; a new "finger-molded" plastic steering wheel in 1968; wire wheel covers, chrome side scoops, and a revised T-handle shifter in 1969; and a switch to a yellow finish in 1971. The familiar running-horse logo was deleted in 1969; in its place went a decal with the number 535 beneath the Mustang name. AMF finally shut down its pedal car assembly line in 1972.

According to Ken Schmidt of Blue Diamond Classics, a leading pedal car dealer in Indianapolis, AMF built 118,712 kid-pow-

The truly young buyer was a prime target of Ford's marketing campaign in the 1960s. Plastic model Mustangs were very popular, and kids who had a few more dollars to spend could have opted for a larger, motorized scale replica of their dads' favorite pony car.

ered Mustang convertibles, all using the same stamped steel body modeled after the real thing. After ceasing production in 1972, AMF sold its tooling to the CIA Corporation in Mexico City. There, Mustang pedal car production resumed, this time in various colors. An attempt to revive the breed came in 1984 when The Little Car Company of San Diego tried to import 1,000 pedal cars from the Mexican firm to help commemorate the full-sized Mustang's 25th anniversary. Poor quality hindered the effort. Only 200 were distributed among dealers here in America.

All Mustang pedal cars, whether born in the United States or Mexico, are valued collectibles today. According to Schmidt, a CIA-marketed pedal car, new in its box, can bring at least $650. AMF-built examples in excellent condition can sell for twice that price.

The K-code Hi-Po 289 was rated at 271 horsepower. Installing this engine option also required the Special Handling Package and 6.95x14 tires. Also notice the generator on the left—a sure sign that you're looking at a 1964-1/2 Mustang. Alternators were used beginning in 1965.

Opposite: Most missed the small addition made to the 289 fender badge on Mustangs like this 1964-1/2 convertible. The two small words on top read "High Performance." The "Hi-Po" 289 became an option in June 1964.

Two weeks before the Mustang's April 1964 introduction, Captain Stanley Tucker, an airline pilot from St. Johns, drove by his hometown Ford dealership and noticed a Wimbledon White Mustang convertible on display. The car had been touring Canada on special loan from Ford to promote pony car sales north of the border. Tucker saw it, then bought it, becoming not only the first Canadian to own a Mustang, but the owner of the very first Mustang too. Unbeknownst to the dealer and Tucker, the white convertible wore serial number 100001—it was Job One. Ford officials had intended to show it off in Canada, then bring it back home for safe-keeping. Forever. The unplanned sale, of course, changed those plans. The 33-year-old pilot liked the car and refused to sell it back to Ford.

Two years and 10,000 miles later, Dearborn officials prevailed, trading Tucker a fully loaded 1966 convertible in Silver Frost paint for the first Mustang.

Serial number 100001 remains proudly preserved today in the Henry Ford Museum in Dearborn. As for the millionth Mustang, it slipped into the dealer network and obscurity, along with Tucker's 1966 convertible.

Other memorable moments for Ford's first-edition Mustang include an appearance at The Brickyard in May 1964 as the prestigious pace car for the 48th running of the Indianapolis 500. The little pony car was also honored with a coveted Industrial Designers' Institute Award. Even more prestigious, at least in Henry Ford II's opinion, was the Tiffany Gold Medal Award bestowed upon the Mustang "for excellence in American design" at the World's Fair press introduction. It was the first time the Walter Hoving, Tiffany & Company had extended this honor to an automobile— though Ford had solicited the award.

Americans simply couldn't get enough of the new pony car in April 1964, nor could they say enough about it. More than 4,000 letters of praise arrived in Dearborn that summer from owners thrilled almost beyond words. Automotive writers faced no shortage of nouns, verbs, or especially adjectives for describing the coveted car.

"A market which has been looking for a car has it now," exclaimed *Car Life*'s review of the new Mustang. "It is a sports car, a gran turismo car, an economy car,

The sleek 2+2 fastback model joined the lineup in the fall of 1964 after 1965 production began. Its base price was $2,553, and production that first year was 77,079. Notice the absence of engine identification on the fender—a standard six-cylinder is beneath the hood.

In the beginning, the 1964-1/2 Mustang relied on a weak-kneed 170-ci six-cylinder for standard power. That base six was then exchanged for a more powerful 200-ci six-holer for 1965. Output went from 101 horsepower to 120 with the larger six.

A standard attraction inside the 2+2 was its fold-down rear seat, which created more usable cargo space. The panel at the rear of the passenger compartment also opened up to extend the "cargo floor" into the trunk. Also notice the functional ventilation louvers in the C-pillars.

a personal car, a rally car, a sprint car, a race car, a suburban car, and even a luxury car." According to *Road & Track*, "The Mustang is definitely a sports car, on par in most respects with such undisputed types as the MG-B, Triumph TR-4 or Sunbeam Alpine." As *Car Life* put it, "The car may well be, in fact, better than any domestically mass-produced automobile on the basis of handling and roadability and performance, per dollar invested."

Clearly Ford designers had met Iacocca's demands, and more. Although the new Mustang shared a lot with the humble Falcon, it did offer the average buyer loads of sporty imagery for a tidy price beginning just short of $2,400. Even with a standard six-cylinder beneath that long hood, the car's clean, crisp looks, working in concert with the standard bucket seat interior, made a driver feel like he or she was traveling in fast company even if he or she wasn't.

The license plate says it all. The battle cry for Iacocca (left) and Frey in 1964 was "417 by 4-17"— 417,000 Mustangs sold by April 17, 1965. The 417,000 figure represented the first-year sales record set by the 1960 Falcon. *Ford Motor Company*

Designer Gail Halderman began working on a third Mustang body style even before anyone asked him to. Once mocked up, no one could deny that the fastback model was a real winner. Notice the classic Studebaker Avanti and E-type Jaguar in the background of this May 1963 photo. *Ford Motor Company, photo courtesy of* Automobile Quarterly

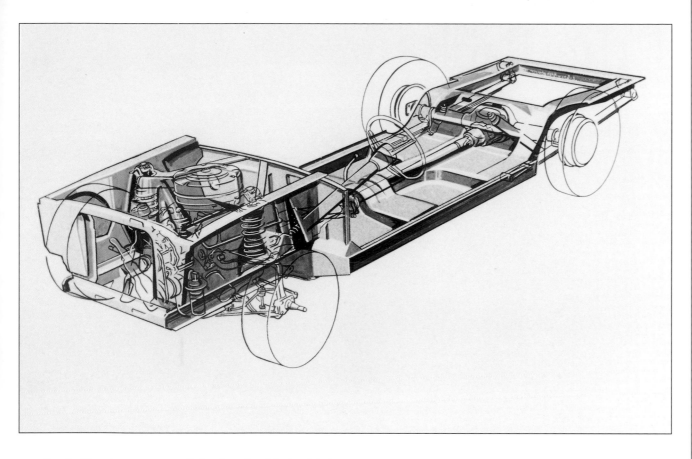

Ford offered more sporty flair when it added a third body style, the 2+2 fastback, to the original coupe and convertible layouts in September. Designed by Gail Halderman, the 2+2 featured an attractive, sweeping roofline and a rear seat that folded down to open up a large, flat cargo floor that extended from the trunk into the passenger compartment. More than 77,000 of these sleek, sexy Mustangs were sold the first year.

Initial power choices early in 1964 included a 101-horsepower, 170-ci six-cylinder, or the Falcon's 164-horse, 260-ci Windsor small-block V-8. A larger Windsor—the 210-horsepower, 289 four-barrel V-8—was also available. This lineup changed as production carried over from 1964-1/2 to 1965 in August 1964. The standard six-cylinder was upgraded to 200 ci and 120 horses, and the 260 was replaced by a 289 two-barrel V-8 rated at 200 horsepower. More compression boosted the 289-4V small block to 225 horsepower for 1965.

The really big news came in June when Ford offered the promised High Performance 289. Easily the highest-priced Mustang option at $328, the "Hi-Po" 289 represented just the ticket for drivers who wanted to back up those sporty impressions with real performance.

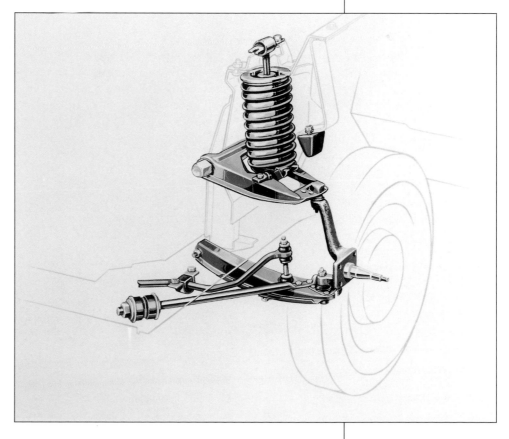

Leader of the Pack

Mustangs were seemingly everywhere you looked in April 1964. They were on television. They were at the World's Fair in New York. They were on the covers of both *Time* and *Newsweek*. Maximum public exposure was job number 1 in Dearborn that spring and remained so into the summer. Pony car-crazed Americans were flocking into Ford dealerships at a frantic pace as the weather warmed up and Iacocca's marketing blitz showed no signs of cooling down. It actually sped up in May when Ford's first Mustang made yet another prestigious public appearance, this time as the pace car for the 48th running of the greatest spectacle in motor racing.

Each Memorial Day weekend the field of the Indianapolis 500 is led to the starting line by a production-based pace car. The maker of that pacer then proudly commemorates the moment by offering street-going replicas to the public. While Chevrolet currently leads the way with the most lead laps run (12) at The Brickyard, it is Ford that probably deserves credit for originating the modern Indy pace car replica. In May 1953, Dearborn shipped 2,000 fully loaded, specially identified "Official Pace Car" Sunliner convertibles—all done in Pace Car White—to dealerships to help mark both Ford's first postwar Indy 500 pace-lap assignment (Ford's actual first appearance at Indy came in 1935) and the company's 50th anniversary. Many dealers then furthered the promotion by replicating the replicas themselves.

Dodge copied Ford's trick with its own run of specially painted and lettered pace car replicas in 1954, as did DeSoto in 1956.

Benson Ford pilots the Mustang pace car around the track at Indianapolis at the start of the race on May 30, 1964. A. J. Foyt won the 48th running of the Indy 500 in his Offy-powered Mickey Thompson special, making it the last victory for a front-engine roadster. *Indianapolis Motor Speedway Archives*

Interestingly Chevrolet passed up its chance to do the same in 1955. Chevy's first Indy pace car promotional push didn't come until the new Camaro debuted in 1967. A second Camaro, the restyled 1969 model, also paced Indy. Chevrolet marketed pace car replicas in both instances: about 100 in 1967, 3,675 in 1969.

Ford waited eight years between Indy 500 appearances. A gold Thunderbird convertible paced the field in 1961. Then along came the Mustang and another golden opportunity for Dearborn officials to show off in high-flying fashion.

The Mustang was barely six weeks old when it hit the bricks on May 30, 1964. Three actual pace cars were specially prepared for race day—two of these serving as back-ups in case of an accident or parts failure. Another 35 Festival Cars were delivered to Indianapolis to handle parade

Ford also built full-roofed Indy pace car replicas as part of the "Checkered Flag" contest, which awarded one of these coupes to the 105 best salesman in the dealership network. All the winners pose here with their cars in Dearborn on May 14, 1964.

chores. All of these Mustang convertibles, the 3 pacers and 35 parade cars, were painted Wimbledon White with Indy pace car graphics and blue racing stripes supplied by the 3M Company.

The three pace cars were fitted with all the race-day extras common to Indy pacers. Two flag stanchions were added in back and three grab handles—two beside the rear seat and one atop the windshield opposite the driver—were bolted in place to help keep pace-lap passengers where they belonged.

There is some mystery concerning the pace cars' mechanical makeup. Most reports claim the three Mustang convertibles were fitted with hopped-up 271-horsepower Hi-Po 289s. Some witnesses think the engines were actually experimental 289-4V small blocks tweaked with various hot components, including parts used by the 271-horse K-code V-8. In any case, these engines were balanced and blueprinted beyond typical Hi-Po specs and their cylinder heads were ported and polished for even greater breathing characteristics. Extra attention was also paid to oiling to guarantee everything stayed together during that one shining moment at 100 miles per hour-plus. A racing-style, wide-sump oil pan was added, as was an oversized radiator for ample cooling capability.

Suspension modifications included a super-stiff front stabilizer bar to help keep things on the level. Cut-down front coil springs and de-arched rear leaves were used to bring down the cars' center of gravity. Also assisting the pace cars in Indy's mildly banked turns were a mismatched set of Koni shocks: 80/20s on the left, 50/50s on the right. Tires were 7.55x14 bias-ply Firestone Gold Lines and brakes consisted of beefed-up front discs and rear drums.

While the 3 pace cars were specially engineered for a triple-digit sprint around the track, the 35 festival cars were better suited to hauling petite race queens and the like at much slower speeds. These all-

Mustangs have led the pace lap at Indy twice since 1964, each time in honor of a totally new pony car. The first Fox-chassis Mustang (center) toured the Brickyard in 1979, followed by the redesigned 1994 Mustang 15 years later. *Indianapolis Motor Speedway Archives*

show/no-go parade vehicles were standard-issue Mustang convertibles fitted with D-code, low-compression 289-4V small blocks. Some had four-speeds; some had Cruise-O-Matics. Reportedly all were sold after the race at a dealer auction in Louisville, Kentucky.

The fates of the three pace cars remain nearly as much a mystery as their under-hood makeup. Some stories claim the car driven by Benson Ford on race day in May 1964 was given to that year's winner, A. J. Foyt, and later wrecked. According to Indy officials, however, all three pace car convertibles were returned to Ford after the race. From there, the trio reportedly went to the Holman-Moody race shop in North Carolina. Holman-Moody then definitely delivered one to Sebring, Florida, for pace car duty there; another perhaps to Watkins Glen, New York, for the same job. If the third car was not given to Foyt and later wrecked, it may have been sent to California, possibly Riverside, also to serve as a pace car. Only one of the three, the Sebring car, has since resurfaced.

As many as 190 (perhaps more than 200) replica coupes were also built in April and early May 1964. These Mustang pace cars featured the same lettering and racing stripes as their convertible counterparts, but were painted Pace Car White instead of Wimbledon White. All of these were outfitted in the same way: F-code 260-2V V-8, Cruise-O-Matic automatic, power steering, and white interior.

Ford returned to The Brickyard 15 years later to pace the 63rd running of the Indy 500. This time, the company established an all-time high for pace car replica production, rolling out 10,478 copies of the car that Jackie Stewart drove around the track on May 27, 1979. Of that total, 5,970 were fitted with 2.3-liter four-cylinders and four-speeds, 2,402 had the 5.0-liter V-8 backed by a four-gear, and 2,106 featured a 5.0L/automatic combo. All were painted Silver Metallic with black accents and red/orange striping.

Yet another redesigned Mustang was honored with Indy pace car duties after another 15-year wait in 1994. This time Ford's Special Vehicle Team supplied three mildly modified Cobra convertibles for race day and another 1,000 replicas for sale to the public. All were painted Rio Red and were powered by a pumped-up version of the Mustang GT's 215-horsepower 5.0-liter small block that produced 25 extra horses. Adding the official pace car lettering on the outside was up to the buyer—many didn't.

Three times in 36 years—when will the Mustang lead the pack at Indy again? Sooner than 2009, we hope.

One of the Mustang's earliest sales promotions came in May 1964 to help mark the car's selection as that year's Indianapolis 500 pace car. Dearborn awarded 105 pace car replica coupes to this country's top-selling Ford dealers. Here Lee Iacocca hands over one of those cars to Mr. and Mrs. R. Impellittiere of Cold Springs, New York. *Ford Motor Company, photo courtesy of* Automobile Quarterly

Known also by its engine code—"K"—the High Performance 289 pumped out 271 horses, which didn't kick in until 6,000 rpms. The engine could wind out another thousand rpm without complaint.

The Hi-Po 289 featured strengthened main bearing caps (fastened down by two bolts, not four) holding a nodular-iron crankshaft. Typical cast-aluminum 289 pistons were tied to the crank by beefed rods with reinforced "big ends" clamped down by large 3/8-inch bolts. Helping keep a K-code small block smooth at high rpm was a larger harmonic crankshaft balancer measuring 1 13/16 inches thick, as opposed to the standard 1-inch thick balancer.

Durable valvetrain pieces included stiffer dual valve springs and hardened pushrods, spring retainers, and keepers. Standard cast rocker arms were mounted firmly in place by screw-in rocker studs; other 289s used press-in studs. Additional K-code components installed with high-rpm operation in mind included a larger pulley (3.875 inches, compared to 2.75 inches) for alternator-equipped Hi-Po 289s and a special, stronger fan

with increased pitch to maximize cooling capabilities.

Feeding the Hi-Po was a 600-cfm Autolite four-barrel on a typical 289 cast-iron 4V intake. A solid-lifter cam actuated standard 289 valves. A mechanical-advance, dual-point distributor fired the mixture. And special free-flowing, cast-iron exhaust manifolds helped speed spent gases on their way. Topping things off was a chromed, open-element air cleaner, a low-restriction piece that both looked great and did its job as designed.

The K-code option included the Special Handling Package (quicker steering and stiffer springs, shocks and sway bar) and a set of 6.95x14 nylon "Red Band" tires. A three-speed manual was standard behind the Hi-Po, with a four-speed option available at $184. An optional automatic wasn't mated to the 271-horse 289 until 1966. This beefed-up Cruise-O-Matic transmission was priced at $216, not too much to pay to let the non-shifting set in on the fun.

The Hi-Po Mustang with optional 3.89:1 gears went 0–60 in 8.3 seconds. It covered the quarter-mile in 15.9 seconds at 85 miles per hour. Armed with

4.11:1 gears, *Hot Rod's* test subject lowered the 0–60 time to 6.9 seconds and tripped the lights at the far end of the quarter-mile in 15.5 seconds.

The K-code 289 remained the Mustang's top performance option through 1966. It carried over briefly into 1967, but was by then overshadowed by the 390 GT big-block V-8. Hi-Po production was 7,273 in 1965, 5,469 in 1966, and only 472 in 1967.

Ford offered other options, performance and otherwise, to help make the Mustang many different cars for many different buyers. You name it—deluxe interior appointments, a console, air conditioning, power assists for brakes and steering, a power top for convertibles, wire wheel covers, a vinyl roof, racing stripes, a tachometer, and so on—it was available for buyers willing to spend a little, or a lot, more. Along with looking so cool, it was the pony car's wide-ranging versatility, something totally unexpected from an affordable compact, that contributed to its instant success in the marketplace. And its longevity.

Some 35 years later, Americans are still talking about Mustangs.

Airline pilot Captain Stanley Tucker of St. Johns, Newfoundland, inadvertently became the world's first "Mustanger" when he bought pony car Number One from a St. Johns dealer, who didn't know the car in question was only for show. Tucker later traded his Wimbledon White convertible for the 1,000,001th Mustang built. *Ford Motor Company, photo courtesy of* Automobile Quarterly

The one-millionth Mustang rolled off the Dearborn assembly line at 11:02 A.M. on Wednesday, February 23, 1966. Lee Iacocca (back to camera) is holding the door as Donald Frey enters.

CHAPTER 3

HAPPY TRAILS?

Mustang Ups and Downs, 1965–1973

The key to the pony car's unprecedented success right out of the box was what Lee Iacocca called "the three faces of Mustang." It was this "split personality" that set Ford's new breed apart from every other small, affordable automobile then on the road. In base six-cylinder form, the Mustang was a frugal, practical economizer. If a customer checked off all available comfort and convenience options, he or she received a relatively luxurious "mini-T-bird." And last, but certainly not least, adding the 271-horsepower Hi-Po 289, Special Handling Package, and other musclebound pieces transformed Ford's spry pony into a real racehorse.

The attraction of the latter two "faces," the luxury showboat and macho musclecar, were enhanced even further in April 1965 with the introduction of two new option packages, the Interior Decor and GT Equipment groups. The GT package offered both a nice collection of performance imagery pieces and a decent dose of real performance. The work of designer Damon Woods, the Interior Decor option added simulated wal-

nut accents and special seat inserts featuring a herd of galloping horses—thus the nickname "pony interior."

Clearly Mustang customers had a choice, and they kept on choosing more and more as the years rolled by. Buyers who stood pat with the budget-conscious six-cylinder/three-speed combo were in the minority from the beginning. Six-cylinder installations made up 35.6 percent of the 1965 run and 41.7 percent of the 1966 run. But from there the optional V-8s took over big time. The six's percentage fell to 30 percent in 1967, 18.4 in 1969, and 9.8 in 1971. Standard three-speed sticks made up 31.9 percent of the 1965 mix, then dropped to 17.2 in 1969 and to 10.8 in 1971. Meanwhile, option choices as a whole continued rising. The typical amount spent on extras per car went from $358 early in 1964 to more than $500 by 1967.

It was then that the Mustang began to depart from Iacocca's original ideal, as the once-svelte pony car continued growing bigger and heavier after 1966. Redesigns in 1967 and 1971

Above: Deluxe interior features also grew in prominence in 1967, as demonstrated by this flashy console with its large enclosed storage bay. Also present here is the optional Stereosonic AM radio/eight-track tape deck.

Left: Lee Iacocca may not have liked what happened to his little baby after 1966, but buyers were definitely impressed with the improvements made to ride and handling. They also didn't mind the extra power supplied by the Mustang's first big-block V-8, which fit so nicely within the car's widened flanks up front.

Introduced along with the GT package in April 1965, the Interior Decor Group offered a touch of class for Mustang cockpits. Included was simulated wood grain paneling for the dashboard, a sporty five-dial instrument cluster in place of the dull Falcon instrumentation, a simulated walnut steering wheel, bright pedal trim, and pistol-grip door handles. Courtesy lights (barely visible behind the driver seat) were also added to the door panels.

increased parameters and made the Mustang less like a sporty compact and more like a touring sedan. More luxury also became part of the equation, as did more power. Engines accordingly grew bigger and heavier.

Reasons for all this growth were varied, although Ford believed it was simply responding to the wishes of the masses. Customers wanted more, so more was what Dearborn gave them. Purists could complain as loud as they wanted about Ford "ruining the Mustang" after 1966. They were still overwhelmingly outnumbered by satisfied buyers—at least in 1967. In 1971 it was a much closer call. By then, even loyal customers were complaining.

Two other factors played major roles in the direction the Mustang took after 1966. The first involved competitive pressures supplied both by the various rival pony cars that began showing up in 1967 and yet another new breed of American automobile that had initially debuted in 1964. The former group included

Above: Mustang fans today know the Interior Decor option as the "pony interior." The name comes from the running-horse seat inserts added front and rear as part of the package.

Far left: A sporty addition for any 1965 Mustang, six-cylinder or eight, was the Rally-Pac tach/clock combo. Priced at $69.30, the Rally-Pac mounted atop the steering column. It was available through 1966.

Left: A tilt steering wheel became an option in 1967. Pushing the turn signal lever forward allowed the wheel to move up and down through nine different positions. The tilt wheel also swung up and over when the door opened, to allow easier entry and exit for the driver.

By Any Other Name

The Mustang was Ford's most popular export for many years. Shipments overseas started shortly after the confetti settled here in America in April 1964.

Dearborn officials had to jump through various hoops to get the cars out of the country as motor vehicle import regulations varied around the world. To be sure exported cars could handle rough roads, Ford equipped all Mustangs sent overseas with heavy-duty suspensions.

Cars with V-8 power were fitted with a one-piece V-shaped brace (in place of the standard two-piece setup) that more effectively tied both shock towers to the firewall beneath the hood. Shelby Mustangs also took advantage of this stronger reinforcement, which quickly became known as the "export brace."

Apart from a few other minor modifications, all export Mustangs were essentially identical to those built for U.S. roads. All save for those delivered to West Germany. The firm Humbold-Klockner-Dautz already claimed the rights to the name "Mustang" in that country. H-K-D was a veteran manufacturer of marine engines, locomotives and diesel trucks, and it reportedly was planning a "Mustang" truck in 1964. H-K-D officials offered to sell Ford its rights to the name for $10,000, but Dearborn officials passed on the deal. Instead the West German car was marketed as the T-5, the code originally used for the pony car development project in 1962. The word *Mustang* was removed throughout the car, but the running-horse symbol was left on the grille, fenders, and glovebox door. Some of the cars had speedometers marked in kilometers.

A few extra tweaks were needed whenever a T-5 was ordered with the GT Equipment Group or Decor Interior. Solid rocker stripes were fashioned for the GT T-5 to fill in the space left black by the removed "Mustang" block letters. The gas cap also simply read "GT." For the pony

When was a Mustang not a Mustang? When it was exported overseas. A German company in the 1960s already owned the rights to the Mustang name, so cars shipped overseas were stripped of all such identification. For lack of a better name, the T-5 code was used instead. T-5s were exported throughout the 1960s into the 1970s. This T-5 convertible is one of 151 built for 1967. Notice the fender badge.

Like their American counterparts, T-5s could've been ordered with six-cylinders or V-8s. However, all exported models were fitted with heavy-duty suspension and a special V-shaped brace that tied the shock towers more firmly to the cowl. Thus, this one-piece unit became known as the "export brace."

No, T-5s weren't any faster than American Mustangs. This speedometer reads in kilometers per hour, not miles.

interior application, the wood-grain steering wheel was fitted with a blank center. Some Decor Interior T-5s were simply fitted with the standard steering wheel with a blank center.

In later years, Ford made additional changes to the West German T-5s. These included revisions to the turn signals and rear license lamps, the color of the high-beam indicator light, and the parking brake.

Other Euro-style features such as headlight flashers, large driving lights, a larger-capacity fuel tank, and a locking ignition switch were also added to some cars.

A German-language owners manual was printed for the T-5. English counterparts were used too, because so many American servicemen in West Germany bought the cars. The manuals for U.S. military personnel were standard items with a rubber-stamped message on the cover reading, "In consideration of trademark rights in Germany: T-5."

Many of the cars delivered to American soldiers overseas eventually found their way back to this country because both owners and their cars were given free rides home once tours of duty were up. West German laws also made it difficult to sell American automobiles on the used-car market over there.

T-5 production numbers are not known. Ford Export reportedly stopped using the designation in 1977, so even T-5 variants of the Mustang II were created. The only known English-language T-5 sales brochure, printed in 1971, mentions Grandes, Mach 1s, and even Boss 351s, all stripped of their full names for delivery to West Germany. According to this brochure, "Mach 1 '71 is a fantastic road car you can only see coolly tooling down the Autostrada to Rome or the Autobahn to Munich."

A Mustang by any other name was still a Mustang.

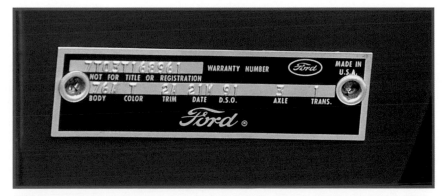

T-5s were tagged with Domestic Special Order (DSO) codes in the 90–99 range, which of course signified export sales. Most, like this 1967 model, wear a 91 DSO code.

Right: Ford advertising people were definitely ahead of their time when they began specifically targeting young women in 1966. This famous ad also fit in with Iacocca's "three faces of Mustang" plan. Keeping the car's appeal as wide as possible was the key to its record-setting sales pace.

Below: Ford planners made more than one push to promote six-cylinder sales during the Mustang's first-generation run. Sprint models combined budget-conscious practicality with just enough style and flair to keep things interesting.

Far right: Freshened treatments for the grille and side scoops and new "Mustang" fender script identified the 1968 Mustang. The body was an identical carryover from 1967. *Steve Statham*

A new body debuted in 1969, as did two high-profile options: the "Shaker" ram-air hood scoop and revamped styled-steel wheel. The fastback body also became a "SportsRoof" that year.

Chevrolet's Camaro and Pontiac's Firebird. The latter featured the high-performance machines inspired by Pontiac's 1964 GTO. High-horsepower musclecars quickly became all the rage after "the Goat" made the scene, and Ford designers knew they had to keep up or give up. They also knew that GM's pony car knock-offs would feature room enough up front for powerful big-block V-8s. Thus they went back to the drawing board to find a way to shoehorn an optional big block between Mustang flanks. The car's first big block, the 390-ci FE-series V-8, debuted in 1967. Two years later, even bigger big-block Mustangs were running with the fastest, most powerful musclecars ever to roll out of Detroit.

Then there was Bunkie.

Semon E. Knudsen, "Bunkie" to friends and foes alike, had first made a name for himself by reviving Pontiac after taking over as general manager there in 1956. A decade later, he also became the main man behind both the Mustang's rise to power in 1969 and the breed's second ballooned body in 1971. Although he was only at Ford for 19 months, he alone did more

The California Special was a Shelby knock-off created by Southern California dealers in 1968. A similar "Shelby-ized" High Country Special was also marketed by Colorado Ford dealers that year. *Ford Motor Company, photo courtesy of* Automobile Quarterly

to stir up the pony car pot than everyone else in Dearborn combined. And he managed to piss off everyone else in Dearborn to boot—including Lee Iacocca and Henry Ford II.

Henry II was at first overjoyed. He wasted little time shocking everyone in Detroit by hiring the veteran General Motors executive in February 1968 after Bunkie had resigned in a fit because Ed Cole was made GM president over him. "Henry was a great GM admirer," recalled Iacocca in his autobiography. "For him, Knudsen was a gift from heaven. Perhaps he believed Knudsen had all that famous GM wisdom locked in his genes. In any event, Ford wasted no time in making his approach. A week later, they had a deal. Knudsen would take over immediately as president at an annual salary of $600,000—the same as Henry's."

As the man Henry II passed over to hire Knudsen, Iacocca had every reason to be upset. He even briefly considered doing to Ford what Bunkie had done to GM, but then he decided to stick around and watch. Maybe Knudsen wouldn't work out, he thought. Good

thinking. The GM defector almost immediately managed to step on toes everywhere he went in Dearborn.

On top of that, Bunkie also kept pushing Ford products in a direction contrary to what his boss had in mind. Knudsen valued racing and performance and demonstrated this thinking by introducing the wild and wooly Boss 302 and Boss 429 Mustangs in 1969. Apparently, in Bunkie's mind, the Mustang only needed one face, a strong one. And, in keeping with that thought, he also sponsored the 1971 redesign, a project that made even more room up front for even more engine.

By then, however, the days of big engines and high horsepower were all but over. The musclecar was history. Safety crusaders, insurance agents, and tailpipe sniffers had seen to that. Seemingly everyone in Detroit in the late 1960s knew the end of era was upon them, except for Bunkie. "He was a racing nut, but he failed to understand that the heyday of racing had passed," said Iacocca.

On September 11, 1969, Henry Ford II fired Bunkie, this after warning him more than once that he

Special FX

In the early 1960s, big Fords were serious contenders at the track. Full-sized Galaxies dominated NASCAR stock car racing in 1963, and they were no slouches in the quarter-mile. Dearborn designers even went so far as to build special lightweight Galaxies for professional drag racers in 1962, 1963, and 1964. There was also the race-only version of the 427 FE big block, the "high-riser," with its monstrous ports, to speed things toward the winner's circle. This bruiser was joined by the exotic single-overhead-cam (SOHC) 427, the so-called "Cammer," in 1964. Originally created with superspeedways in mind, the Cammer went on to become the scourge of National Hot Rod Association (NHRA) dragstrips in 1965 after being legislated out of contention in stock car racing by NASCAR mogul Bill France.

Ford drag racers in 1964 were also treated to a new way to travel 1,320 feet in a hurry. This time the car was the midsized Fairlane, which, when Dearborn Steel Tubing was finished with it, became the lightning-quick Thunderbolt. Mid-11-second blasts down the quarter-mile were no problem thanks to about 480 horses worth of 427 high-riser stuffed beneath a weight-saving fiberglass hood. Atop that hood was a huge teardrop-shaped scoop required to clear the high-riser's dual four-barrels. In back, a gnarly Detroit Locker differential with stump-pulling 4.56:1 gears was held in place by large, welded-on traction bars.

Additional pounds were trimmed by adding plexiglass side windows and molding the fenders and doors out of fiberglass. Early Thunderbolts also were fitted with a front bumper and splash pan made of fiber-

glass. These two items were later traded for aluminum pieces.

Ford needed to build only 50 Thunderbolts to qualify them for NHRA stock-class competition, but 127 were eventually let loose on the competition. One of these lightweight Fairlanes, driven by Tasca Ford's Bill Lawton, copped Super Stock honors at the 1964 NHRA Winternationals. Another, piloted by Gas Ronda, won the NHRA Top Stock World Championship that year.

Lawton's Tasca Ford team, from East Providence, Rhode Island, traveled cross-country to Pomona, California, again in 1965. And Lawton made it all worthwhile by taking another Winternational title. This time the class was Factory Experimental (FX), the newly formed catch-all category created to keep up with the growing number of so-called factory super stocks coming out of

This is how an A/FX Mustang factory drag car looked when the guys at Holman-Moody were through with it in 1965. Renowned restoration man Randy Delisio left Dave Geiger's piece of Ford performance history in its plain Poppy Red wrapper upon completing its reconstruction in 1992.

A/FX Mustangs were fitted with 427 SOHC or 427 hi-riser V-8s in 1965. Twin four-barrels were originally bolted on top, but they were commonly replaced by injectors.

Detroit. Fiberglass fenders were one thing. Solid front axles, acid-dipped bodies, and altered wheelbase (for improved weight transfer during launches) couldn't be considered "stock," super or otherwise, no matter how you looked at it. Chrysler had begun showing off such radical tricks in 1964, just in time for drag racing's sanctioning bodies to adjust the rules to stay ahead of the escalating factory drag car battles.

Ford, of course, had no choice but to retaliate after some pretty wild Mopar machines, most notably Dick Landy's altered A/FX Dodge, appeared on the scene in 1964. The Thunderbolts then became dinosaurs almost overnight, convincing factory-backed teams like Tasca Ford to just as quickly trade horses. The car Lawton spurred on to the A/FX title in 1965 wasn't a Fairlane, it was a Mustang.

It was only logical that Ford start placing its drag-racing bets on its wildly popular pony car. After all, the term was *Total* Performance. Pursuing Henry Ford II's quest for dominance of the racing world, the company invested millions of dollars in an Indy 500 engine project that resulted in a win at The Brickyard in 1965 and the GT program that would eventually garner Le

Mans laurels in 1966. While obviously successful, neither of these efforts demonstrated any real ties to what the typical Ford fan drove home from the race. Drag racing, on the other hand, presented the opportunity for at least stock-*looking* cars to compete. And compete they would as long as Lee Iacocca had anything to do about it.

"We will stay in open competition as long as we feel it contributes to better automobiles for the public," he said in late 1964. "It's estimated that 43 million people a year now go to motorsport events. We may be old fashioned, but with that many people in the stands, we figure it's a pretty good place to show how well our products can perform in direct competition with the products of other manufacturers."

To make the Mustang competitive in NHRA and AHRA competition, this time Ford chose the not-so-little race shop run by John Holman and Ralph Moody in Charlotte, North Carolina. A "prototype" A/FX Mustang was built in Dearborn and shipped to Holman-Moody, where the H-M crew then used their experience to improve on what Ford engineers had done.

Owner Dave Geiger had his A/FX Mustang put back into its original racing form a few years after its restoration. *Dave Geiger*

In all, Holman-Moody built 15 A/FX Mustangs in 1965. These fastbacks showed up in Charlotte without powertrains, hoods, fenders, or doors. The only glass installed was the sloping rear window. H-M men first stripped the chassis of all stock suspension components. Specially fabricated jigs were then used to make the transformation from stock-bodied Mustang to all-out drag racer a snap.

One of the more radical modifications involved reworking the rear wheel wells and nearby floorboard section to move the axle 3 inches forward. This put more weight on the slicks during hard acceleration. Rear quarter panel sheet metal then needed altering too. Wheel openings were reshaped to allow clearance for all the extra, relocated rubber. Additional body mods included plexiglass windows and fiberglass fenders, hood, and doors. With these lightweight parts a completed racer weighed about 3,200 pounds.

Suspension work was every bit as extensive. A special cross-member was added in back to serve as a mounting point for traction bars that were welded on to the axle housing at their trailing ends. Extensions of these arms also ran backward behind the axle to a point near the leaf spring shackles. There, these extensions served as mounting points for an extra set of shock absorbers. In front of the axle, mounting braces for the traction bars were drilled for five different locating points. Bolting the traction bars into the uppermost holes resulted in a "no load" setting. Each hole down preloaded the rear suspension to a higher degree. This allowed the cars to be set up specifically for the traction conditions of each track.

Front suspension work was even more radical. The shock towers were air-chiseled out to make room for the 427 big-block; steel plates were welded into the upper third of each opening, and brackets were then welded on to these plates to supply mounting parts for shortened upper A-arms. In place of the deleted stock coil springs went a pair of two-leaf flat springs that worked like torsion bars. These springs ran straight back from the front "frame horns" to the lower A-arms.

Wheels were American mags, skinny 4-inchers in front, 6-inchers in back wearing 10-inch M+H slicks. Supplying the heat to melt that M+H rubber was an SOHC 427 fed, in some cases, by twin four-barrels. Cammers were initially in short supply in 1965, so only 7 of the 15 A/FX Mustangs were originally fitted with the overhead-cam 427. The other 8 received 427 high-risers, although most were later refitted with a Cammer once one became available.

On the track in 1965, Gas Ronda set an NHRA A/FX record in his altered Mustang, turning in a 10.43-mile-per-hour/134.73-mile-per-hour time slip. The A/FX Mustang shown here, one of four known survivors, was originally delivered to Larson Ford in White Plains, New York, in the plain Poppy Red wrapper supplied by Ford. Bob Hamilton did the driving. The car was soon repainted blue, and injectors were added to the Cammer in 1966.

NHRA officials that year modified their rules concerning altered-wheelbase cars, and most of the A/FX Mustangs were returned to Holman-Moody to have their rear suspensions relocated to the stock position. New rear-quarter sheet metal was installed, and the extra shocks in back were removed. This particular Mustang did not make it back to the H-M shop and thus still sports its original altered wheelbase. The car was brought back to life by noted restorer Randy Delisio in January 1992. Owner Dave Geiger later had the original Larson Ford graphics restored too.

Today this gorgeous restoration stands as a proud example of just how wild a Mustang could be in 1965.

Suspension modifications were radical at both ends. Long control arms were added in back with an extra pair of shock absorbers bringing up the tail.

needed to change his aggressive ways to work in Dearborn. Some claimed Knudsen was trying to take over. Iacocca had another explanation for the short-term president's quick demise: "I wish I could say Bunkie got fired because he ruined the Mustang or because his ideas were all wrong. But the actual reason was because he used to walk into Henry's office without knocking. That's right—without knocking!"

With Knudsen knocked out, the door was left open for Iacocca, who then helped fill the void along with two other executives in a "troika" arrangement. Finally, on December 10, 1970, Iacocca was made the lone president, a position that two years before he thought he'd never see. Fortunately he chose to stay at Ford and watch Knudsen fail, a result he wasn't alone in rooting for. "The day Bunkie was fired there was great rejoicing and much drinking of champagne," he remembered. "Over in public relations, one of our people coined a phrase that soon became famous throughout the company: 'Henry Ford once said that history is bunk. But today, Bunkie is history.'"

As much as Bunkie Knudsen did to transform the Mustang into a boulevard brute in 1971, blaming him completely for the breed losing its youthful figure isn't entirely fair. After all, the pounds had started piling on before he arrived.

Designers first began drawing up a plumper pony even as the original was galloping away with the attentions of an entire nation in the summer of 1964. Meanwhile, if-it-wasn't-broken-don't-fix-it was the plan for 1966. Save for trim adjustments and an updated grille, the 1966 Mustang appeared nearly identical to its forerunners. The car also established an all-time production high for Dearborn's pony car legacy: 607,568 cars.

Although Iacocca later complained about the Mustang's growth, he did oversee the 1967 redesign, which he hoped would carry on in the tradition already established.

Refinements beneath the skin were the responsibility of chief engineer Tom Feaheny. His team did their best to improve ride and handling by revising the front suspension geometry. Steering effort was also reduced while precision was increased.

Increased as well were nearly all measurements. While the wheelbase remained at 108 inches, overall length (183.6 inches) and width (70.9 inches) were stretched by 2 and 2.7 inches, respectively. Overall

height went up nearly an inch to 51.8, and the track increased 2 inches to 58 at both ends. Both interior and trunk space grew, as did the all-important engine compartment. All this growth in turn meant more weight, 140 pounds to be exact for the base six-cylinder coupe. On the outside, the 1967 Mustang was viewed by most critics in its day as a nice upgrade of the image, and the base price was still less than a dollar a pound.

That price grew as well when the new optional big block was dropped into the widened, reinforced engine bay. The 320-horsepower 390 Thunderbird Special V-8 cost $263.71 in 1967. What those dollars translated into on the street was only a modest increase in performance. But it was a start, and a whole host of truly hot big-block pony cars would follow soon enough.

Another restyle in 1969 added more heft to the body as width and length again increased. Weight went up markedly too. Fortunately, for the aesthetic-minded, the top continued to drop, contributing to a new look that came off nicely sleek despite the extra inches. Especially attractive was the new SportsRoof, Ford's equally new name for the fastback. SportsRoof accents included such sport-minded touches as simulated rear-quarter air intakes and a ducktailed spoiler in back. The supreme SportsRoof rendition—at least at introduction time in the fall of 1968—was the

Mustang performance began flourishing in 1969 as the Mach 1, Boss 302, and Boss 429 were introduced. But also new that year was a different breed of pony car, the luxury-minded Grande. Shown here is a 1970 Grande with the optional vinyl roof. *Ford Motor Company, photo courtesy of Automobile Quarterly*

It was a small, affordable car named after a horse, and it was introduced on April 17. Sound familiar? Actually, the date was April 17, 1969, and the name was Maverick. An even smaller Ford product, Pinto, followed two years later to further signal a new downsized direction for the Better Idea guys. Downsizing the Mustang then came in 1974. *Ford Motor Company*

Mach 1, introduced for 1969 to take the Mustang's sporty image another step higher. When equipped with the sizzling 428 Cobra Jet big block, itself introduced midyear in 1968, the Mach 1 instantly became one of Ford's toughest musclecars.

The two Boss SportsRoofs, the 302 and 429, didn't make their debuts on the street until January 1969. The Boss 302 was a small-block screamer best suited for tight turns, while the Boss 429 simply had no business being on any street, straight or curved. It was a race car plain and simple.

Also debuting in 1969 was a fourth new model, the Grande. Available as a hardtop only, the Grande was created to promote the Mustang's second face, its soft, luxurious side. Special exterior trim and a deluxe interior with simulated wood accents were among the list of classy standard features. Underneath, voided rubber bushings were installed into the leading mounts of each leaf spring in back to better absorb road shock. A special insulation package with 55 pounds of extra sound deadener material was also installed to help make the Grande, in Eric Dahlquist's words, "as quiet as Jack Benny when the check comes to the table."

Grande production figures indicate just how much Mustang buyers had grown to love the car's softer side. After building 22,182 in 1969, Ford rolled out another

13,581 Grandes in 1970. But then things turned around after Bunkie's big body appeared for 1971. Grande production that year jumped to 17,406, then 18,045 in 1972, and 25,274 in 1973. That last figure represented 19 percent of the 1973 run. The 22,000-odd Grandes in 1969 made up only 7.4 percent of that year's total. Clearly something had changed the way buyers looked at their Mustangs. Could that something have been the fall of high performance?

Ford was out of the go-fast business almost entirely by 1971. While a few surviving musclecars remained in the pipeline early in the year, the days of truly powerful engines were over, as was the life span of the big-block Mustang. Once the end arrived, the question was not how far the mighty had fallen but how quickly.

In 1969 the number of engines available to Mustang buyers hit an all-time high at nine. Among these were 302 and 351 Windsor small blocks, which were enlarged renditions of the old, reliable 289. These were yeoman powerplants. The remaining V-8 lineup featured nothing but mean and nasty muscle mills: the Boss 302, Boss 429, and 428 Cobra Jet. These three

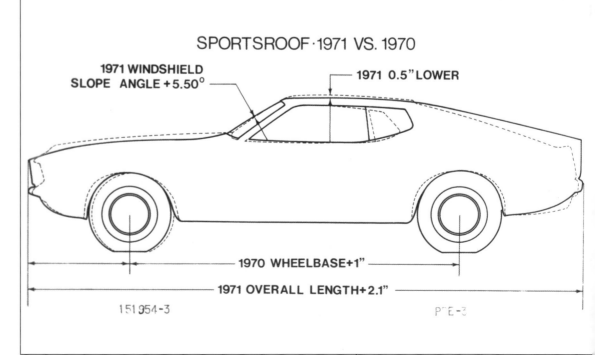

SPORTSROOF·1971 VS. 1970

1971 WINDSHIELD SLOPE ANGLE +5.50°

1971 0.5" LOWER

1970 WHEELBASE+1"

1971 OVERALL LENGTH+2.1"

151954-3

P‍E-3

Bunkie's big baby debuted in 1971, long after he was fired by Henry Ford II. Everything about the 1971 Mustang was bigger, including its top optional V-8. The 428 Cobra Jet, used from 1968 to 1970, was superseded by the 429 Cobra Jet.

high-performance V-8s carried over into 1970 and were joined by a new small block, the 351 Cleveland. The Windsor and Cleveland 351s were briefly listed together, which only served to complicate the long list of Mustang power choices.

Built at Ford's Cleveland, Ohio, engine plant—thus the name—the 351 Cleveland shared only its displacement with the old 351 Windsor, which was manufactured in Windsor, Ontario, as you might have already guessed. The Cleveland small block was the product of Ford engineers' efforts to create lighter, cleaner-running, more efficient V-8s with better economy and lower emissions. With its free-breathing, canted-valve head design, the 351-2V (two-barrel) Cleveland put out 250 horsepower. The four-barrel Cleveland made 300 horses in 1970.

Cleveland small blocks were considered performance engines, yet they used two-bolt main bearing caps instead of the preferred, more durable four-bolt caps

normally designed into high-revving, high-horsepower engines. Cylinder heads also varied between the 2V and 4V variations. Two-barrel heads had small valves (2.04-inch intakes, 1.66-inch exhausts) and were of the "open-chamber" design. Four-barrel Cleveland heads featured wedge-shaped combustion chambers and larger valves—2.19-inch intakes, 1.71-inch exhausts.

Built for the future, the 351 Cleveland had a future. Ford's other performance engines didn't, especially after Dearborn closed down its race shops. On November 20, 1970, Ford Motor Company sales group vice president Mathew McLaughlin announced that Ford was pulling out of all motorsport activities, with the exception of limited support for drag racing and off-road competition. Dearborn's mighty racing program—the force behind the Total Performance campaign, the support for high-performance research and development, the reason behind a number of hot-to-trot Fords hitting the street—was history.

In 1960, Iacocca began pushing Ford to jump on the youth market bandwagon. Ten years later, the members of that market were older and wiser, and the sales-conscious marketing marvel was paying close attention to changing attitudes. Performance was taking a bad rap, from those who feared it as a threat to innocent women and children and those who could no longer afford the high cost of horsepower. In Lee's mind, racing had become a bad investment.

Out as well were many of Ford performance's movers and shakers. Special Vehicles director Jacque Passino resigned the day before Thanksgiving 1970. By that time the Boss 302 Mustang had been killed; the Boss 429 had been cancelled earlier in the year.

Not all was lost, however. One last Boss Mustang remained, if only because of the availability of the 351 Cleveland. Using Cleveland small-block power, the 1971 Boss 351 was every bit as impressive as its two race-bred Boss forerunners while offering more

in the way of tractable street manners. But it lasted only one year.

One other last stand for Mustang performance came in 1971, this one courtesy of Bunkie Knudsen. In February 1968, Bunkie had needed just one look at Gail Halderman's mock-up to give the go-ahead for the final expansion on the long-hood/short-deck theme. None of the other candidates mattered. Bunkie had his mind made up. By 1971 the Mustang would be bigger and better—and faster—than ever.

Complaints about interior room and comfort did have something to do with the 1971 Mustang's growth, but the main impetus was supplied by the new cleaner-running 385-series big-block V-8, introduced in 1968. The 385-series 429 was lighter than its FE predecessor, yet wider thanks to its canted-valve heads. To replace the Mustang's 428 Cobra Jet—its days numbered due to ever-tightening emissions restrictions—the socially acceptable 429 would require an enlarged engine bay.

The 1972 Olympic Sprint convertible was put together for Washington, D.C., area Ford dealers to commemorate the 1972 Olympics and the capital's annual Cherry Blossom Parade. Only 50 of these patriotic convertible Mustangs were built that year.

The Race Is On

At no time in automotive history has so much of the competition been caught with its pants down as when the Mustang burst on the scene. Plymouth's Barracuda barely scratched the market that the Mustang ripped wide open. The "417 by 4-17" battle cry in 1964 wasn't bravado. Iacocca, Frey, and the rest knew all along it was money in the bank. The Barracuda might have arrived first, but there's a reason why they call them all pony cars—the Mustang showed everyone else in Detroit how it was done.

Mustangs continued galloping on with no fear in 1965. And 1966. Plymouth's glass-backed Valiants found 60,188 buyers in 1965, the high-water mark for the entire 1964–1974 run. By 1966, Ford was selling nearly that many Mustangs every six weeks. Then came 1967.

General Motors first sent word down from the top to start developing its own pony car in August 1964. Curiously, Chevrolet chief designer Irv Rybicki had proposed a new small, sporty Chevy, something similar to Ford's early Thunderbird, as early as 1962, but it was shot down by, of all people, Bunkie Knudsen, then the division's general manager. Bunkie changed his mind two years later after the Mustang

forced GM's hand. The go-ahead was given for Chevy's F-body platform, and the Mustang's arch-rival was born three years after that. Chevrolet general manager Pete Estes unveiled the Camaro to the press on September 12, 1966.

Not only did Chevy's new pony car mirror the Mustang in every way, it also went one step beyond with a big-block V-8 option that for the first time had Iacocca's baby eating dust. The 1967 SS 396 Camaro, announced in November 1966, was both a pony car and a musclecar. Dearborn's 390 GT Mustang, also introduced that year, was just a pony. Chevrolet gained even more ground in the performance pony car field that same month by rolling out the fabled Z/28 Camaro. It was two years before Ford came back at Chevy with a "Trans-Am" pony car of its own, the Boss 302 Mustang.

Pontiac made it a three-car race after introducing its equally legendary, aptly named, Trans Am Firebird in 1969. Today, the flashy T/A remains the only musclecar to have rolled uninterrupted from the 1960s into the 21st century. But both GM's F-bodies, Camaro and Firebird, are teetering on the brink, with rumors circulating of their imminent demise. Meanwhile, the Mustang gallops on.

Pontiac Motor Division's pony car project began life as a true sports car, the two-seat "Banshee" dream machine engineer John DeLorean and then general manager Pete Estes had been considering as early as 1963. DeLorean continued working on his sporty ideal after his rise to the g.m. seat following Estes' move to Chevrolet in July 1965. Work on the Camaro was already under way, but DeLorean would have nothing to do with the F-body platform. He was still toying with a two-seater as late as February 1966.

Then GM Executive Vice President Ed Cole stepped in. In March 1966 he ordered DeLorean to forget about the Banshee and "make a car out of the Camaro." The 1967 Firebird then debuted on February 23, 1967. Like the Camaro, it too was available in hot big-block form. And it too could run away from a 390 Mustang.

As if there wasn't enough new competition from GM, Ford Motor Company even copied the Mustang in-house. Mercury's pony car, the slightly longer, more prestigious Cougar, appeared in 1967 and instantly became *Motor Trend*'s "Car of the Year." A truly muscular Cougar, the Eliminator, showed up in 1969 to join the Z/28 and Boss 302.

Two more Trans-Am pony cars showed up in 1970 after Chrysler introduced its new E-body platform for Plymouth's Barracuda and the equally new Dodge Challenger. Hemi-powered E-bodies ranked among the quickest musclecars of all-time. But the best all-around performers were the SCCA race-ready AAR 'Cuda and T/A Challenger, both powered by triple-carb 340 small

Chevrolet introduced its response to the Mustang, the Camaro, in 1967. Chevy that year also rolled out a new kind of pony car, the Z/28, a Trans Am–inspired road rocket that could run circles around all rivals. Rally wheels and black stripes were the only Z/28 giveaways in 1967.

1967, 317,404 in 1968, 299,824 in 1969, and 190,727 in 1970. Firebirds likewise bit into the pony car pie and continued to shine during the disco years, when the garish Trans Am was as fashionable as a lime-green leisure suit. Firebird production was 211,453 in 1979, more than half of which—117,108—wore "screaming chicken" Trans Ams livery.

Mustangs survived such attacks, finding even more buyers than the Trans Am. Sales of the redesigned Fox-chassis Mustang surpassed 365,000 in 1979. Camaro, Firebird, 'Cuda, Challenger, and Javelin simply made the pony car race that much more interesting.

Pontiac too joined the pony car ranks in 1967 with its Firebird. The fabled Trans Am followed two years later. Today, the Trans Am stands as the only musclecar to roll uninterrupted from the 1960s into the next century. In 1999, Pontiac marked three decades of consecutive service with a special 30th anniversary Trans Am (rear). In between is Detroit's last great musclecar, the 1974 455 Super Duty Trans Am.

Even American Motors got into the pony car race. AMC's Javelin was exciting enough on its own, but the company's movers and shakers still went one step beyond to create the two-seat AMX. *Chrysler Historical Archives*

blocks. Even in plain-Jane form the E-body Barracudas and Challengers of 1970 to 1974 had among the sportiest images in the pony car market.

Once-frumpy American Motors jumped on the pony car bandwagon in the fall of 1967 with its attractive new Javelin. AMC's unique two-seat AMX then appeared in February 1968. Hoods didn't come any longer, nor decks any shorter than those found on the stumpy AMX, which AMC group vice president Vic Raviolo called "the Walter Mitty Ferrari." These sporty two-seaters were offered through 1970, then the AMX and Javelin names were joined together atop AMC's conventional pony car lineup. Like Chrysler's E-bodies, the Javelin retired after 1974.

All the competition had an impact on Mustang sales. Production numbers dropped each year after the zenith, 607,568, was reached in 1966 as Camaro popularity took root. Ford built 472,121 Mustangs in

The Olympic Sprint's red, white, and blue exterior treatment was complemented by similar interior appointments.

Luxury was a major selling point in 1973. Mustang convertibles that year received knitted-vinyl seat inserts and molded door panels. The large console and three-spoke deluxe steering wheel shown here were optional.

The 1971 Mustang was nearly 3 inches wider than the 1970. Its track was also widened by a whopping 3 inches, front and rear. Wheelbase was stretched an inch, and overall length went up by 2 inches. Weight increased by about 400 pounds. Anyone with eyes could see how much bigger this baby was compared to its predecessors. And the gains were especially evident in the 1971 SportsRoof with its nearly flat rear roofline.

Rearward visibility was exceptionally poor for the SportsRoof Mustangs of 1971 to 1973. But who needed to look back, at least in 1971, when all that bulging hood in front was hiding the optional 429 Cobra Jet big block? The 370-horse 429 Mustang represented Knudsen's final legacy, and it also stood tall as one of the quickest pony cars—make that Fords—ever built. Yet it too was cancelled after a brief run.

After 1971, all that remained for the discriminating Mustang buyer was the 351 Cleveland and the Grande. Then they retired, along with the first-generation Mustang, at the end of the 1973 model run. Ford's pony car would never again be so many different cars for so many different drivers.

The last of the first-generation Mustangs was treated to a new grille/headlight layout and a new bumper in 1973. A wide array of options could also be added to dress up a 1973 Mustang. Tape stripes, a blacked-out grille, a chin spoiler, and the ram-air hood appear here.

Air conditioning, full instrumentation, AM-FM stereo—it didn't get much better as far as pony car drivers were concerned in 1973. This particular 1973 convertible includes roughly $1,600 in options—a figure representing about 50 percent of the car's base price.

PUTTING THE SPURS TO THE PONY
GT Mustangs, 1965–1969

It was the Mustang's first birthday, but it was Ford customers who got all the presents. You might say it was Dearborn's way of thanking all the little people for their overwhelming support. On April 17, 1965—12 months and more than 417,000 pony cars after the long-hood/short-deck craze officially began—Ford announced the availability of two new options packages to help enhance the Mustang's image even further. As if it needed it.

One of these new additions to the 1965 options list was the snazzy pony interior with its galloping-horse seat inserts and simulated walnut paneling. The other was the "GT Equipment Group," a nice combination of sport-minded form and function that helped revive at least some of the fun-loving nature that many critics felt Ford had sadly neglected while transforming the two-seat Mustang I into a more practical regular-production reality. From 1965 to 1968, GT Mustangs represented the flashy, frisky flagships of the fleet. No other American car offered as much blood-pumping pizzazz for the money, at

least not until Chevy's Camaro, Pontiac's Firebird, and Mercury's copy-cat Cougar debuted in 1967 to begin stealing more and more of the GT's thunder. GT Mustangs were briefly offered one last time early in 1969 before they were completely overshadowed by their own brethren, the newly introduced Mach 1, Boss 302, and Boss 429.

In 1965 and 1966 there was nothing else in the small car ranks like the GT Mustang. Turbo Corvair? Too small and unconventional, if not "un-American." Formula S Barracuda? Too obscure: few but the Plymouth faithful noticed. And the Mustang was better value than the Barracuda, or any of Detroit's other sporty offerings. The Formula S package, which included Chrysler's 273 four-barrel V-8, added $258 to the price of a $2,586 V-8 Barracuda in 1965. A Mustang V-8 hardtop that

Above: A "GT" gas cap was a new addition to the GT Equipment Group in 1966.

Left: The flagship of the Mustang fleet from 1965 to 1968 was the hot-to-trot GT, with its sport-minded suspension and high-profile imagery. GT production continued up through 1969, but the cars were overshadowed that year by the Mach 1, Boss 302, and Boss 429. Shown here is a 1966 GT fitted with the optional Hi-Po 289.

Fender emblems and lower bodyside stripes were included in the GT deal in 1965. The always-attractive styled-steel five-spoke wheels were optional. Disc brakes were standard, but power assist was not included.

year cost $2,426—$2,321 plus $105 for the 289 Windsor small block. Ford's GT package added $165 more. The V-8 GT option did not include the motor, but required buyers to purchase one of two four-barrel V-8s. "Standard" in the GT was the 225-horse Challenger Special 289, at a cost of $53 over the base V-8. Thus, a hardtop Mustang GT ($2,321 + $165) with the 225-horse 289 V-8 ($105 + $53) cost buyers $2,644, or $200 less than the $2,844 Formula S Barracuda.

Drivers who truly wanted to get their kicks in a GT Mustang could reach up to the top shelf for the K-code High-Performance 289 with 271 rarin'-to-race horses. While the Hi-Po 289 cost $328 for "typical" Mustangs

in 1965, it was a $276 option when ordered along with the GT Equipment Group—this because the K-code engine option included some of the same chassis components already included in the GT package.

Pony car buyers could add the GT package to all three 1965 Mustang models. Typical "base" price for a GT convertible that year was $2,828, while a GT fastback cost $2,804 without any additional options. With the GT package, Mustang owners received a decent dose of Euro-style Gran Turismo imagery. But there was more to the GT Mustang than sporty looks.

The V-8 GT equipment deal included the Special Handling Package.

On its own the Special Handling Package was a $30 option available for any non-GT Mustang in 1965. This option, in typical 1960s fashion, simply stiffened up things underneath. Spring rates increased from 82 to 105 in-lb in front, and 101 to 130 in-lb in back to help improve on the original Mustang's weak-kneed road-holding characteristics. Limiting body roll even further was a thickened front stabilizer bar, a 0.84-inch unit in place of the wimpy 0.69-inch standard Mustang bar. Another Special Handling feature was quicker 22:1 steering, compared to the standard ratio of 27:1. Optional power-assisted steering also used the faster 22:1 ratio.

Revalved shocks and stiffer springs didn't exactly represent chassis engineering at its finest, from today's perspective that is. Yet it was the best Ford people could do in 1965. And these improvements did limit much of the inherent rocking and rolling that had left many journalists in 1964 complaining of this so-called sporty car's unsporty ride.

Writing about the standard suspension and brakes introduced in 1964, *Road & Track*'s testers found "The ride is wallowy, there's a tendency for the car to float when being driven at touring speeds and the 'porpoise' factor is high on an undulating surface."

The same *R&T* guys turned an about-face later in the year after getting their hands on a Hi-Po 289 Mustang. "Knowing the 'power team' to be well proven, we were most interested in trying out what is referred to in Detroitese as the 'handling package,'" read *R&T*'s September 1964 report. "The effect is to eliminate the wallow we experienced with previous Mustangs, and to tie the car to the road much more firmly, so that in a fast turn the point of one's departure into the boondocks is delayed very considerably. There is a certain harshness to the ride at low speeds over poor surfaces, but this is a small price to pay for the great improvement in handling and road holding."

As for the faster steering box, it too represented a marked improvement. "Naturally, the handling package introduces a certain amount of ride harshness, but its effect on the steering is almost purely beneficial," concluded an October 1964 *Car and Driver* report. "The 'quick' steering ratio is still too slow by our standards, but with the revised suspension it feels taut and stable, and on high-speed curves (with relatively small steering wheel movement) it's highly satisfactory."

Early GT Mustangs could be identified easily by their fog lamps and corresponding grille bar. These lights were controlled by a toggle switch found low on the far left of the dash.

Like the pony interior option, the GT Equipment Group in 1965 included the five-dial instrument panel. And since this car is also equipped with a pony interior, the instrument panel is done in simulated walnut. The fog lamps' toggle switch can be seen to the left of the steering wheel.

Front disc brakes were also part of the GT performance lineup. These 10-inch ventilated discs put a stop to additional critics' complaints about the wimpy drums used at all four corners on standard Mustangs. As *Road & Track* explained in its May 1964 issue, "Present drums (nine-inch diameter on sixes, 10-inch on V-8s) have 212 square-inches of swept area for the six, 251.3 square inches for the V-8, and represent (with steering quickness) the major area where Mustang still cannot match the European sports car."

"An optional power booster reduces pedal pressure by over 50 percent," added *Car and Driver*, "but the brakes have nothing like adequate fade resistance—four consecutive complete stops from 80 mph reduces braking efficiency dramatically."

The GT's appearance package carried over in similar fashion into 1967 with the one major exception involving the fender badge, which was now located within the lower bodyside stripe. Power assist for the front disc brakes was included this time around.

New for 1967 was this designation. The red "A" stood for automatic transmission. Manual trans cars were simply GT Mustangs, while automatic models were GTAs. This was the only year this badging was used.

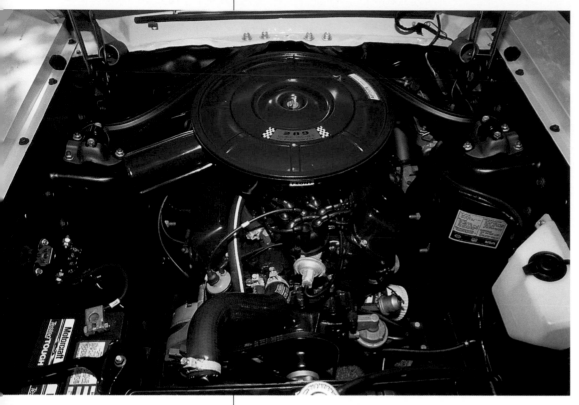

While only four-barrel-fed V-8s were available for GT Mustangs in 1965 and 1966, a 289-2V was allowed into the fraternity in 1967. More appropriate power choices included the new 390 big block, the High-Performance 289, and the 225-horse 289-4V, shown here.

Later in 1964, *Car and Driver* reported on the disc brake option: "With all the performance, it's comforting to know that the brakes are now fully able to cope with both emergency stops and repeated stops from high speeds. The Kelsey-Hayes ventilated disc brakes on the front wheels passed our fade tests and simulated panic stops easily, while pedal pressure and travel remained constant. These brakes should be standard equipment on all high-performance Ford products." Indeed.

Power assist wasn't offered along with the front disc brake option, which cost $57, when ordered by mere mortal Mustang fans not opting for the GT options group.

The Hi-Po 289 breathed through low-restriction dual exhausts. The other 1965 GT Mustang V-8, the 289-4V, sent spent gases into the atmosphere via a single tailpipe in standard non-GT applications. At the ends of either GT V-8's dual exhausts were chrome trumpets poking through cutouts in a special rear valance panel. Those cutouts displaced the standard bumper guards normally located in those positions.

When optional dual exhausts were ordered for any V-8 Mustang, they required the addition of spot-welded

reinforcement plates at the tail end of each unit-body "frame rail" in back. While the presence of these reinforcements does not necessarily help document a true GT Mustang in 1965 and 1966—remember, optional duals were available for non-GTs too—their absence on a car in question means it is not a factory-built GT no matter how many other GT features are present. Anyone today can transform any early Mustang into a GT with all the right parts.

Ford promotional people muddied those waters by offering nearly all GT appearance features (everything save the actual "GT" emblems) as over-the-counter dealer options not long after the GT Equipment Group option was introduced. Thanks to all this promotional exploitation, a "factory-correct" 1965 Mustang could have looked very much like a GT but not actually been one. Full-page ads in 1965 even spelled out the situation in no uncertain terms: "Make your Mustang into a GT! Your Ford dealer has the goods."

Along with all its mechanical muscle, a true factory-built Mustang GT in 1965 featured lower body-side GT stripes with widely spaced "Mustang" block letters located at the trailing edge of each front fender. The standard "Mustang" lettering and running-horse logo normally found a bit higher up on those fenders were replaced by "GT" emblems. Up front, a unique grille bar framed by fog lamps at each end joined the familiar running-horse "corral." Those lamps, along with the exhaust trumpets out back, were the prime features added by dealers as part of Ford's "Make your Mustang into a GT!" promotion. The stripes were available separately as well.

Completing the GT package was a five-dial instrument panel in place of the standard Falcon-style dashboard layout. Instead of the conventional left-to-right-sweeping 120-miles-per-hour speedometer braced by too-large fuel (left) and temperature (right) gauges, the five-dial GT instrumentation put a racy, round 140-mile-per-hour speedo directly in front of the driver. On each side were a pair of real gauges: smaller round readouts for fuel and temperature remained to the far left and right, respectively, while between them and the speedometer were an oil pressure gauge (left) and an ammeter (right). Non-GT drivers in 1965 relied on "idiot lights" to let them know too late when lubricant was low and the battery wasn't charging.

The pony interior option included the same five-dial instrument panel with one difference—it was adorned with a simulated walnut applique. The GT five-dial panel was done in camera-case black. Both were trimmed out in chrome Mylar highlights.

When the five-dial instrument panel (with slightly different trim) became a standard feature for all Mustangs in 1966, it helped bring down the price for the second-edition GT package to $152. Included in this price was a new "GT" gas cap. Not included were the bright rocker moldings that also became standard Mustang features in 1966. Like the rear bumper guards, they were superseded when the GT Equipment Group was ordered. The 1966 Mustang's revised grille was also blacked out. All other GT pieces carried over from 1965.

A sporty option that just begged to become part of the GT appeal also reappeared in 1966. Ford's beautiful chromed 14x5 styled-steel wheels fit the sporty image to a T, although the $119.71 asking price in 1965 probably convinced most GT buyers to stick with conventional wheel covers. The same could be said in 1966 even though the price dropped to $93.84—that was still a lot of green back then. Original-edition styled-steel wheels are sometimes mistakenly identified today as being part of the original GT package, but that's undoubtedly due to the fact that seemingly every restorer out there refits a GT Mustang with a set of these gleaming spokers.

Restoration experts over the years have also commonly added a second option, the Rally-Pac, into the GT mix. Introduced about a month after the Mustang debuted, the Rally-Pac featured two black-crinkle-finish pods, the one on the right housing a 24-hour clock, the left a 6,000-rpm tachometer. The two pods fit saddle-style atop the steering column, just where they needed to be to ensure good visibility. The option was available for six-cylinders and V-8s and was priced at $69.30—again a hefty price, especially considering that front discs cost almost 15 bucks less.

When ordered along with the Hi-Po 289, the 6,000-rpm tach was traded for an 8,000-rev unit. Another variation involved the unit's marriage to the five-dial dashboard in April 1965, this because the original setup would have partially obstructed the driver's view of the 140-mile-per-hour speedo, as well as the oil pressure gauge and ammeter. A revised, low-profile Rally-Pac was then introduced for the GT cockpit and its pony interior counterpart. These were black crinkle too, although some were painted to match the color of the steering column. Both original and low-profile Rally-Pacs were sold in 1965, depending on instrument panel installation. The latter type then of course took over completely in 1966 after the five-dial dash became standard. The Rally-Pac option price that year remained the same as in 1965.

The price for the GT package in 1967 jumped to $205.05 as a set of F70x14 Wide Oval tires became part of the deal. Mounted on 6-inch wide stamped-steel wheels in place of the 5-inch rims used on 289-powered non-GT models, these fat treads from Firestone featured an 8.45-inch cross section and were adorned with white sidewalls. The cross section for the standard 14-inch black sidewall Mustang tire was only 6.95 inches. Next up was the optional 7.35x14 rubber. Wide Ovals could be added optionally to any V-8 Mustang in 1967 in exchange for an extra $62.35. Also still available for all Mustangs were those classy five-spoke, styled-steel wheels, which once again qualified as suitable icing for the GT cake.

Whether mounted on the gleaming optional wheels or the conventional standard rims, the new Firestones represented a step in the right direction for a road-ready pony car that many felt was just then coming into its own. "In short, just about every Mustang change for '67 seems to bring the car closer to our notion of a true Grand Touring machine," wrote *Motor Trend*'s John Ethridge after driving the third-edition GT Mustang. Ethridge, of course, was referring to the sum of the parts—the 1967 Mustang's widened, reinforced body, restructured front suspension, and big-block power influx all contributed to a higher level of performance that was then accentuated further by the GT options group. But he also couldn't put a final period to his December 1966 review without mentioning how well the wide treads worked with the improved chassis. "Of course, the Wide-Oval tires put more rubber on the ground and contribute to overall traction," he pointed out. "With ride and handling thus improved, this second-generation Mustang can boast a new surefootedness."

The rest of the GT equipment list in 1967 looked much like the one published in 1966. Working in concert

Opposite: The GT package was offered for all three Mustang body styles during its five-year run. This 1967 GTA fastback is also fitted with the optional lower back panel, a ribbed grille priced at about $20.

A standard gas cap with "GT" identification was included in the 1967 package, but could be superseded by a pop-open cap when the Exterior Decor Group was added.

with those Wide Ovals was a heavy-duty suspension that again tightened things up underneath. Beefier shocks and the thickened 0.84-inch front sway bar were joined by less-willing springs that were 30 percent stiffer up front, 26 percent in back. Front disc brakes returned, only this time they did include power assist. Fog lamps were again in the grille, a "GT" pop-open gas cap appeared at the tail, and GT stripes once more graced the lower bodysides, as did new "GT" badges within the stripes' forward sections. No "Mustang" lettering was used.

Badging represents one of the most noticeable areas where 1967 GT makeup differs from its 1966 predecessor. For this year only, Ford's image-makers chose to set GT Mustangs apart depending on transmission choice. Manual transmission cars wore the familiar "GT" identification, while automatic-equipped models were adorned with "GTA" badges (with the "A" in red) at the bottom of each front fender. Gas caps in either case, stick or automatic, still read "GT."

Perhaps a bit less noticeable at a glance, yet of far more importance, was the issue of GT engine availability, which also took a right turn toward the big time. The Mustang's new optional big block, the 320-horsepower 390 Thunderbird Special 4V V-8, joined the 289 4V and Hi-Po 289 small blocks as available GT power sources in 1967. At the other end of the scale, the mundane 289 2V small block, rated at 200 horsepower, was also added to the list, doubling the number of engine choices offered to GT buyers that year. As in 1965 and 1966, the four-barrel V-8s were all three fitted with dual exhausts capped off by chrome tips (quad outlets this time) as standard GT fare. But the two-barrel 289 remained in single-exhaust form when installed in a 1967 GT Mustang. Clearly Dearborn officials wanted to widen the GT's scope in an effort to entice both Clark Kent and his alter-ego.

Engineers, on the other hand, were still doing their darndest to keep their wildest pony kicking. New for 1967 was an LPO (limited production option) package

The Hi-Po 289 was on its last legs in 1967. In its place for GT buyers was the 390 big block, rated at 320 horsepower.

ened or beefed. Basic upgrades to the standard Mustang chassis in 1967 did manage to improve both ride and handling at the same time—a seeming physical impossibility in most minds back then. But achieving GT-type handling required a compromising GT-type ride.

Automotive writers praised Ford's efforts to improve handling, with certain qualifications. After flogging a 225-horse small-block GT, *Road & Track's* crew wrote, "Coupled with the taut foundation of the Mustang is handling that, if not particularly responsive, is predictable, stable and safe." Make no mistake about it, though, the Mustang with the 289 engine is still a very front-heavy car. But it is a car you can drive with flair on a winding road. The steering, which becomes a bit truckish at city speeds, is pleasantly accurate in its feedback of information from the tires. Although we wished for quicker steering, it's easy to see why Ford no longer offers it with this package—the steering effort would be unacceptable to 99 percent of its customers, including us."

Straight-line performance for the 289 4V GT qualified as nothing to write home about. According to *Road & Track*, 60 miles per hour from rest arrived in 9.7 seconds and the far end of the quarter-mile showed up after 17.4 clicks at a lukewarm 84 miles per hour. The Hi-Po 289 GT naturally promised better numbers, but no one tested this rare breed in 1967, the last year for the 271-horse small block. The 390 big block, however, was another story. This was the muscle-bound torque mill both Ford fans in general and the Mustang faithful in particular couldn't wait to read all about. They weren't disappointed, at least not at first.

In its November 1966 issue, *Car and Driver* was among the earliest to publish a road test of Ford's first big-block pony car. "The Mustang 390 GT is as hot as spit on a griddle," claimed the *C/D* scoop. "In fact, it's the fastest of the current crop of sporty-type cars from Detroit—including the Camaro, Barracuda, Marlin, and the Mustang's heavier brother, the Cougar." Acceleration results were 7.3 seconds for the time-honored 0 to 60 run, 7.9 more clicks for the quarter-mile. Trap speed was 91 miles per hour.

Almost everyone else who drove the 390 GT Mustang in 1967 found it to be lacking, certainly as far as its status in Detroit's so-called "supercar" fraternity was concerned. The whole idea behind widening the pony's

only offered to GT customers—and this after they chose either the Hi-Po small block or 390 big block. This race-ready addition, the Competition Handling Package, went more than one step beyond the GT's "standard" heavy-duty suspension. Included were even stiffer springs, a 0.94-inch-diameter front sway bar, Gabriel adjustable shocks, super-quick 16:1 steering gear, a 3.25:1 limited-slip differential, and big 15x6 wheels shod in either 6.50 or 6.70 Goodyear Blue Dot racing rubber.

Also listed as part of the Competition Handling deal were "unique wheel covers." These simulated wires were actually Thunderbird pieces—because the Mustang parts bin carried no 15-inch covers in 1967. As it was, pony car watchers that year hardly noticed the crossover as few GT customers checked off this bone-jarring option. The Competition Handling package's harshness was one contributing factor to its rarity. Its price was another—a whopping $388.53.

The typical GT suspension on its own was enough to keep most mere mortals thrilled behind the wheel while still saving the seat of their pants from any undo wrinkling. Most witnesses agreed the 1967 GT rode noticeably harsher even with the new Mustang's improved platform. Then again, that's exactly what anyone would expect whenever anything underneath is stiff-

flanks to make room for big-block power involved staying ahead of the pack in the horsepower race, and that race wouldn't wait for anyone once it was off and running at full tilt. *Car and Driver*'s early claim concerning spitting on a griddle came before Chevrolet got its 396 Camaro out of the chute in November 1966. The savage 375-horse L-78 version of this little beast appeared shortly thereafter. Plymouth was at the same time rushing its 383-powered Formula S Barracuda to market. These hot-to-trot pony cars, along with Pontiac's fastas-the-wind Ram Air 400 Firebird, were all soon forcing 390 Mustang owners to eat dust. The big-block Mustang, even more nose heavy than its small-block kin, had no advantages over its competitors on the straights or the turns.

The reason for the 390's tepid performance was fairly obvious to those who knew their engine families. While Ford's venerable FE-series big-block lineage included the awesome 427 LeMans engine, the bulk of the group was made up of lazy, loping cast-iron pack mules. Like the 390 ci FE.

In *Hot Rod*'s March 1967 issue, Eric Dahlquist had this to say about the big-block GT: "The best we could do in the 3,419-pound rig was a fair 15.31–93.45, not likely to scare any GTOs or 4-4-2s."

Even the small-block Camaro outran the 390 GT. "Our Camaro 350 was a good half-second quicker in the quarter and 2 mph faster," Dahlquist continued. "But when you think about it, Mustangs have never been very hot in stock form at the track, anyway, just on the showroom floor."

New styled-steel wheels and flashier "C-stripes" adorned the 1968 GT Mustang.

A two-barrel V-8 first became standard for the GT in 1967. A standard four-barrel powerplant returned in 1968, but another 2V small block, this time the 351 two-barrel, again made up the baseline in 1969. Output rating for the 351-2V was 250 horses. Appearing here is the optional 351-4V, rated at 290 horsepower. *Steve Statham*

The last GT Mustang appeared briefly in 1969 before the end came. No fender badges were used this time. Those stripes came in four different colors, depending on paint choice. *Steve Statham*

And when you think about it further, wasn't that what it was all about? Chevrolet or Pontiac people could brag all they wanted about having the fast pony car. Ford's was still the best-selling even after all those rivals debuted in 1967. And GT Mustangs remained a popular choice for pony car buyers who wanted decent doses of prestige, pizzazz, and performance along with their comfort, convenience, and class. All this and they didn't have to break the bank, either.

Was it any wonder then that the 390 GT Mustang copped "best sport sedan over 300 cu. in." honors in *Car and Driver*'s 1967 readers poll? "The Ford Mustang started the whole Detroit sporty-car boom three years ago, and the car has been a gold mine for Ford Division ever since," read the *C/D* announcement of the original pony car's latest claim to fame. "The 289 cu. in. version of the Mustang cleaned up in our poll two years running, and now the heftier, heartier 390 cu. in. GT model is doing the same job."

Speed freaks in 1967 could bitch all they wanted, but they still couldn't dispel the notion that there were few cars out there cooler than a GT Mustang. Apparently image is everything, for Ford's sportiest pony car continued to impress most innocent bystanders as a track star, even though it wasn't. "People are just more aware of the machine than almost anything you can think of being made in America today," wrote Eric Dahlquist about the 1967 390 GT. "Whisking along the freeway at speed or slipping through downtown traffic, heads turn and there is a knowing recognition of being with a winner."

Damn straight. Ford simply couldn't lose with the Mustang GT; it never had a problem getting rid of every one it could build. Production during the car's first half-year run in 1965 was 15,106, followed by 25,517 in 1966. Slower than the competition or not, the 1967 Mustang GT still kept rolling off showroom floors like nobody's business. Sales of the third-edition GT hit 24,078.

That the figure fell to 17,458 in 1968 did not necessarily signal a letdown, it simply reflected the fact that the pony car pie was being sliced up into smaller pieces as rivals began popping out of the woodwork. GT popularity still ran strong, as demonstrated by its cut of total Mustang production. While yearly sales dropped each year after 1966 due to the rise of competing pony

cars, the GT's percentage of those yearly totals kept going up. In 1965 2.7 percent of all Mustangs built were GTs. The portion was 4.2 in 1966, 5.1 in 1967, and 5.5 in 1968.

The price for the GT Equipment Group in 1968 dropped down to its lowest point thus far: $146.71. The absence of power front discs, a $64.77 option that year, accounted for the savings, if you wanted to call it that. Any GT driver worth his or her salt would've probably traded the standard drums for discs anyway, and they were mandatory with the 325-horse 390 4V big block. The "standard" GT engine for 1968 was the 302 4V, rated at 230 horsepower—no two-barrel small block would do this year. Heavy-duty suspension, F70x14 Wide Ovals, and dual exhausts with chrome quad outlets were again part of the plan. The familiar "GT" pop-open gas cap also returned.

Totally new were redone styled-steel wheels, which were the only rims available for the fourth-edition GT. Included in the 1968 package at no extra cost, these 14x6 argent-painted slotted wheels had bright trim rings and small center caps sporting red-painted "GT" identification. Trading the argent paint for chrome plating was optional. These same styled-steel wheels—without the "GT" lettering, of course—were optional for all Mustangs in 1968.

Other GT appearance pieces differed that year. Fog lamps were back, but they no longer were tied together with the horizontal grille bar. "GT" badges rode higher up on each front fender as the rocker stripes were exchanged for flashy "C-stripes" running from the headlights to just behind the door. GT customers left living in the past could've opted for 1967-style rocker stripes instead of the large C-stripes. And those who preferred a high profile at night could've shelled out for the Reflective Group, available only for GT Mustangs in 1968. The GT stripes and paint on the styled-steel wheels became highly reflective by way of this option.

The 1968 GT once more looked the part of a high-performance machine, but the press again wasn't fooled. Not even the staff at *Car and Driver*. This time they chose to test six of the sporty pony cars side by side: along with the 1968 390 GT, they put the spurs to AMC's Javelin SST, Mercury's Cougar XR-7, Pontiac's Firebird 400, Chevrolet's Camaro SS 396, and Plymouth's 340 Formula S Barracuda. This time, *Car and Driver*'s conclusions put the GT at the tail end of the pack. "It would seem that Ford has been content to rest on its laurels while the rest of the industry has gone all out to win a piece of the Mustang market."

Those words aside, the 325-horse GT still ran third fastest in the group, this despite being powered, in *C/D*'s words, by "a bit of a stone" in the old 390 FE V-8. The 0–60 clocking was 6.3 seconds, the quarter-mile e.t. read 14.8 seconds at 94.6 miles per hour. The 325-horse Camaro, the 325-horse Cougar, and the 315-horse Javelin all turned in slower times. But both the Barracuda and the 335-horsepower Firebird beat the horse patties out of the Mustang, the latter running a sizzling 14.1-second quarter (at 100.3 miles per hour) and a 5.5-second 0–60 sprint. The 275-horse small-block Barracuda also did 0–60 in 5.5 seconds but took two more tenths to complete the quarter-mile. Terminal velocity through the lights was 99.1 miles per hour.

Content no more, Ford engineers introduced a truly hot GT Mustang in April 1968. This car was still powered by the aging FE-series big block, but this FE was the 428 Cobra Jet, a 335-horsepower concoction that had Eric Dahlquist literally screaming about the fastest production car he'd ever driven. His famous March 1968 *Hot Rod* test of an early super-stock model resulted in a quarter-mile time of 13.56 seconds at 106.64 miles per hour. (For more on this street performance legend, see chapter 6.)

All 428 CJ Mustangs were GT models in 1968. In 1969 the 335-horse king of the Ford performance corral became available for non-GTs and GTs alike. Priced the same as in 1968, the 1969 edition of the GT Equipment Group again featured a two-barrel V-8 in standard form, only this time it was the enlarged 351 Windsor small block, rated at 250 horsepower. Additional GT power choices included the 290-horse 351 4V, the 320-horse 390 4V, and the Cobra Jet, with or without ram-air equipment. As in 1967, dual exhausts with chrome quad outlets were included in the GT package, but only behind the four-barrel V-8s.

Stiffened underpinnings, this time called the GT Handling Suspension, were again included. So too were the "GT" pop-open gas cap and the argent styled-steel wheels. Changes for 1969 included E70x14 Wide Oval belted tires and the return of the GT rocker stripes, these done in four colors (black, white, red, or gold)

depending on exterior paint and interior color choices. Racing-style hood pins were new, as was a nonfunctional hood scoop with integral turn signal indicators. This fake scoop was swapped for a fully functional, through-the-hood "Shaker" when the ram-air 428 Cobra Jet was installed.

Missing was the typical "GT" identification found on the fenders of earlier models. Only the gas cap in back and the styled-steel wheels' center caps carried "GT" identification in 1969. Few probably noticed, though, because the last of the GT Mustangs came and went early in the year with nary a "so long, glad to know ya." Only 5,396 1969 GTs were built, all of them overshadowed by the two new Boss Mustangs and, more important, the Mach 1. The latter machine instantly took over the role of high-profile leader of the Mustang pack and never looked back.

As for the GT, it would be 13 years before those two letters would again be used with the word *Mustang* in the same sentence.

The last of the first-generation GT Mustangs came standard with a nonfunctional hood scoop and racing-style tie-down pins. Total GT production in 1969 was 5,396.

VARIATIONS ON THE THEME
Carroll Shelby's GT 350 and GT 500

One can only wonder what would've become of Ford's Total Performance campaign had veteran racer Carroll Shelby made it big as a chicken rancher. Obviously Lee Iacocca and crew wouldn't have closed up shop had Carroll decided to do his business elsewhere. But it's certainly safe to say that the Blue Oval banner might not have waved nearly as high as it did without Dearborn's short and happy relationship with the Shelby American works in Southern California. When it came to promoting the "Powered by Ford" label, nobody ever did it any better.

And to think it all started simply enough in 1962. All Shelby wanted was to build his own racing machine. He had the car: the British-built AC Ace. Ford had the engine: the all-American 260 small block. As Shelby quickly proved, the English body fit the

Windsor V-8 like a glove—a boxing glove, that is. The resulting Shelby Cobra packed a punch like nothing ever seen before from an American manufacturer. Then the 260 was replaced by the 289, which in turn was topped by the super heavyweight, the 427. High-performance legends loom no larger than the unbeatable 427 S/C Cobra, easily the fastest "production" car ever produced in this country. Eat your hearts out, Corvette lovers.

The venomous Cobra struck so quickly and successfully, it made Shelby a speed legend almost overnight. No one took more notice than Ford. By 1965 the company decided to give Shelby all of its GT development work. He became speed doctor for the British-built Ford GT-40 and for another little project involving one of Ford's own vehicles. Iacocca wanted Shelby to transform the Ford Mustang into a Corvette killer.

"That was the real idea—to go racing. I never wanted to build a lot of automobiles to make a lot of money," said Shelby

Above: A heart condition cut Carroll Shelby's competition career short after a victory at Le Mans in 1959. But within a few years he was back in the racing business, this time as a race car builder. His allegiance with Dearborn began in 1962. He first used Ford power for his outrageous Cobras, then took the Mustang in at Iacocca's request in 1965.

Left: In its original form, Carroll Shelby's GT 350 was a thinly disguised race car. It even came standard in 1965 with naked steel wheels. Optional five-spoke rims supplied by Cragar were available, but why waste the cash if going to the track was the only trip planned? *Steve Statham*

A 34-gallon fuel tank resided in the GT 350R's trunk. The battery and an electric fuel pump were also located there.

As beastly as the first GT 350 was, it still paled in comparison to the GT 350R, which wore no disguise whatsoever—this was an all-out racing machine. R-model Shelby production in 1965 was 36, counting two prototypes.

in a 1971 *Sports Cars of the World* interview. "At the time my intention was to build 100 [Mustangs] a year, because that was what you had to build in order to race." But Iacocca wanted more than that, and what he wanted he usually got. He also was Shelby's main ally at Ford; Carroll wasn't about to say no. "It was Lee Iacocca who really stayed behind us all the way, encouraged us and then he got us into the Mustang program," he said.

So it was that Shelby found himself in the business of building sports-racer pony cars, a move that both made Mustang history and forced Shelby American to trade its original home in Venice, California, for roomier digs adjacent to the Los Angeles International Airport in March 1965. Introduced early that year, the first of Shelby's GT 350 Mustang variants was more racer than sports car, explaining why it remains Carroll's favorite to this day. In his words, the 1965 GT 350 was "a no-compromise car built to get the job done."

All Shelby American had to do was meet the Sport Car Club of America's 100-car production minimum and the company's ready-to-race Mustangs would qualify for the SCCA circuit, where the competition would be E-type Jaguars, Corvettes, and the like in the B/Production class. No problem. Ford supplied the bare-bones

The R-model's Hi-Po 289 was balanced and blueprinted, and its heads were ported and polished. Dyno tests put maximum horsepower at somewhere between 325 and 360.

Far right: The R-model's interior was stripped of everything that didn't matter, including the passenger seat. Headliner, carpeting, upholstery, insulation—it was all dumped.

Right: R-model stopping power was supplied by 11.3-inch front discs.

2+2s from its San Jose plant in Southern California, and Shelby American took care of the rest. GT 350 production began in October 1964, with the official public unveiling coming January 27, 1965.

According to *Motor Trend*, what Shelby did was "take a 2+2, inject some Cobra venom, tone up the leg muscles [and] add lightness." Add lightness? Shelby truly was a magician. By trading the steel hood for a scooped fiberglass unit and deleting the back seat, among other things, Shelby shaved nearly 200 pounds from the car. Rear seating had to go anyway because SCCA B/Production specifications demanded that the car be a two-seater.

As for "venom," that came from a Hi-Po 289 treated to a couple of Cobra-type tricks. Feeding this sneaky snake was a 715-cfm Holley four-barrel on an aluminum intake. At the other end of the internal combustion process was a pair of "Tri-Y" headers leading to glass-pack bullet mufflers that bellowed through short, race-car-style cutout tailpipes exiting directly in front of each rear wheel. Cast-aluminum "Cobra" valve covers and a matching-style oversized

oil pan completed the package. According to Shelby dyno tests, the Holley carb and headers freed up 35 extra ponies. Advertised output for the GT 350's 289 was 306 horsepower.

"Leg muscles" were toned up by adding a thicker 1-inch sway bar up front, override traction bars and suspension-travel-limiting cables in back, and Koni adjustable shocks at all four corners. Handling was aided further by lowering the upper A-arms' mounting points by an inch. Special pitman and idler arms were then required. To help keep suspension geometry precise, the one-piece export brace was used, instead of the stock two-piece arrangement, to tie the shock towers to the cowl more rigidly. A Monte Carlo bar tightened things up even more by spanning the gap between shock towers across the engine, thus triangulating the underhood bracing layout.

Brakes were as-delivered by Ford, but they weren't standard-issue Mustang. All the cars sent to Shelby American were fitted by special order at the San Jose plant with big-car front discs and Fairlane station wagon rear drums. They also arrived with aluminum-case Borg-Warner T-10 close-ratio four-speeds and big, burly 9-inch rear ends installed. The differential was a gnarly Detroit Locker. From there, the remaining modifications were made at Shelby American after the "knock-down" (Ford's term for partially complete) cars were trucked in from San Jose.

What did it cost to have Shelby work his magic on Ford's pony car? As *Car Life* explained, "The Mustang which comes into [Shelby's] grotto costs about $2,300; his tune-up adds $2,200 to that total." And for that price, you didn't even get a color choice or wheel covers. All 1965 GT 350s originally began life on the San Jose line with black interiors and white exteriors. Blue "G.T. 350" rocker panel stripes were added by Shelby. Standard wheels were 15x5.5 station wagon rims wearing 7.75x15 Goodyear Blue dot rubber. Snazzy 15x6 five-spoke Shelby wheels, supplied by Cragar, were available at extra cost, as were Guardsman Blue LeMans racing stripes that ran from nose to tail.

Counting the first street-going prototype, Shelby American built 561 GT 350s in 1965. For years the

The only engine offered by Shelby American in 1965 and 1966 was a High Performance 289, upgraded with a 715-cfm Holley four-barrel and Tri-Y headers. Output was listed at 306 horsepower.

figure was quoted as 562. Then research in 1994 concluded that one of those cars, though planned, was never built. This "missing" Shelby was initially slated to be part of the special run of GT 350 R-models, with the *R* standing for one thing: racing. Shelby American produced two different types of race-ready Mustangs that first year. Along with the R-model road racers, the Shelby hangars were also home to nine GT 350s set up specially for the drag strip. Four more of these drag cars were built in 1966.

R-model production in 1965 was 36, counting two prototypes. There was nothing "street-going" about these cars. They were out-and-out racing machines that could go right to the track without so much as one turn of a wrench—nothing had to go on; nothing had to come off. R-models were delivered from San Jose completely stripped, even more so than their streetside counterparts. No headliners, carpeting, or upholstery.

Left: Shelby's second-edition GT 350 was given a more distinctive identity in 1966, thanks to the addition of rear quarter windows and functional bodyside scoops.
Steve Statham

No sound deadener or insulation. No side glass or rear windows. And no gas tank.

R-model interiors were race car spartan with only one bucket seat, a four-point roll cage, sheet aluminum inner door panels, and a fiberglass shelf in place of the back seat. The stock Mustang dash pad was tossed aside and a six-gauge instrument panel went in place of the original instrumentation. Plexiglass side windows in aluminum frames (without cranking mechanisms) went into the doors, helping slice off some 25 pounds of unwanted weight. Another 20 pounds were deleted by adding more plexiglass in back.

In place of the stock gas tank, the GT 350R received a special 34-gallon fuel container created by joining two bottom halves from standard 16-gallon Mustang tanks. Internal baffles went inside this tank, while a 3-inch snap-open filler cap went on top. Also included was a large "splash cone" surrounding that filler. Joining the tank in the trunk of a GT 350R was the battery and an electric fuel pump.

Additional body mods included covering the rear quarter roof vents and fuel filler in back with aluminum panels. Wheel openings were also reradiused and flared to make more room for a set of wide 15x7 American Racing five-spoke mags shod in Goodyear racing rubber. Both bumpers were left off and a special fiberglass

apron was added up front. It incorporated a large center opening to aid airflow to both a large three-core Galaxie-based radiator and the 289's external oil cooler. Two slots leading to front brake cooling ducts were fashioned into the apron as well. Actually, two different style aprons were used during R-model production, representing just one of various running changes made.

As for power, the standard Hi-Po 289 was taken apart, with the cylinder heads going to Valley Head Service for porting and polishing. All assemblies were balanced and blueprinted, the heads and manifold were port matched, and the whole works reassembled to precise specs. Dyno tests showed output readings of 325 to 360 horsepower for the R-model's small block, which used Cyclone Tri-Y headers and the familiar 715-cfm Holley four-barrel.

These modifications and extra equipment added up to a $5,995 asking price for the 1965 GT 350R, helping partially explain why only 34 were built for "sale to the public." After the two prototypes were put together, Shelby American rolled out three more batches of R-models: the first 15 production examples, followed by five more, then another 14; the last batch was completed in 1966. On the track, the R-model Shelby Mustangs quickly proved their worth, with Shelby American driver Ken Miles piloting one to victory in its first SCCA outing in Texas on Valentine's Day 1965. Shelby Mustangs won the B/Production championship that year, followed by two more SCCA titles in 1966 and 1967.

Even without the R-model modifications, a standard GT 350 in 1965 was still, in *Road & Track*'s words, "pretty much a brute of a car." It was certainly fast in the turns and quick on the straight and narrow—0–60 in only 5.7 seconds, according to *Hot Rod*'s Eric Rickmam. But it was also hard on both the ears and the seat of the pants. It had proven itself to be a real hot number, but was it too hot? Demand for a two-seat, race-ready street machine was obviously limited, as was the car's cost effectiveness. A production run of barely 500 cars requiring extensive and expensive modifications wasn't doing much to reimburse Ford, nor was it supplying the full exposure company officials were looking for. More Shelby Mustangs on the street meant more potential customers would discover what "Powered by Ford" really meant. Thus, Ford directed Shelby to

Interior upgrades for the 1966 GT 350 included the addition of a back seat. Standard features included the Mustang's deluxe steering wheel (with simulated walnut rim), 3-inch competition seat belts, and a 9,000-rpm tach mounted atop the dashpad.

The Hertz Rental Car people added the GT 350 to its rental fleet in 1966; while most of the GT350H models were black, a few other colors, such as this white example, did appear.

The GT350H cars were shod with Magnum 500 wheels with these Hertz Sports Car Club center caps. Production of GT350H reached 1,002 in 1966.

Power for the GT 500 came from a 355-horse 428 fed by two 600-cfm Holley four-barrel carbs. Standard for the GT 350 in 1967 was the same Hi-Po 289 used in 1966 minus the Tri-Y headers. *Tom Glatch*

Opposite: The big block-powered GT 500 joined the GT 350 in 1967. Those driving lamps in the grille were mounted either close together or at opposite ends, depending on state laws where they were sold. Some local laws prohibited the in-tandem mounting shown here. *Tom Glatch*

widen the GT 350's appeal, aiming it more at drivers who took their hot cars a little less seriously.

Retaining a race car image while toning down some of the rougher racetrack characteristics was the goal. For starters, the 1966 GT 350 got a back seat so friends and the family could also enjoy the ride. An optional C4 automatic was made available for those who preferred resting their right arms. And to add a little variety, color choices went from one to five. Joining Wimbledon White in 1966 were blue, red, green, and black. Other exterior mods included different striping and the addition of functional cooling side scoops and rear quarter glass. The latter feature aided visibility and, along with those scoops, helped set the GT 350 apart from the standard Mustang 2+2. Among customer complaints in 1965 was the fact that this $4,500 race car didn't look like much more than a typical Mustang

wearing a few stripes. The new 1966 image was much more distinctive.

Except for replacing the 1965 Shelby's loud cutout exhausts with full tailpipes, the GT 350's power source remained unchanged from 1965. Underneath, however, things were quite different as costs were cut and harshness was lessened. Lowering the front suspension's upper A-arms was discontinued, and the 1965 GT 350's rear override torque control arms were exchanged for simpler underride traction bars. The stiff Koni shocks and that noisy Detroit Locker differential were still around, but were options, not standard. The end result was a GT 350 better suited for the street, yet still ready to hit the track with little fuss or muss. Performance remained hot, and all the Cobra add-on goodies available in 1965 were still at hand for the discriminating lead-footed buyer.

Mystery Motors

Ford designers had widened the flanks of the 1967 Mustang to fit an FE-series big-block V-8 beneath the hood. And if the 390-ci FE fit so easily, then so would its 428-ci big brother. Carroll Shelby's crew quickly proved the benefits of making this jump by rolling out the new GT 500, with its standard 428 big block, in 1967.

But why the 428 and not the even hotter 427 side-oiler? Although Shelby's tweaked 428, at 355 horsepower, was certainly no slouch, it couldn't on its best day compare to the bullet-proof 425-horsepower 427 side-oiler—the powerplant that had brought Dearborn so much success on NASCAR tracks at home and at Le Mans in France. It was the race-ready 427 that Shelby himself had chosen for his legendary, faster-than-hell AC Cobra. The answer was economics. The more plebian 428 was more affordable, more readily available, and more cooperative on the street than the high-strung medium-riser 427.

While a mysterious 427 option—a detuned 400-horsepower 427 with a single four-barrel—did appear in 1968 Shelby American brochures, no 427-powered GT 500 Shelby Mustangs were offered in 1967. At least not "officially."

Witness the "different-looking" 1967 GT 500 shown here. Behind that reshaped grille-opening, beneath that unique triple-striped hood is indeed a 427 big block. Clearly anyone at any time could've performed their own FE swap over the years and certainly many owners or collectors have. Yet a few of the many 427-powered 1967 Shelby Mustangs known today, including this one, are fully documented as being legitimate "factory" creations.

The 427 GT 500 appearing on these pages is the legendary Super Snake, one of the most intimidating Shelby Mustangs ever built. As the story goes, Shelby did indeed consider offering a 427 option for 1967, and this big-block beast was the prototype.

The idea itself actually came from the fertile mind of Don McCain, a former

Various 427-powered 1967 GT 500s are known, but there is only one *Super Snake*. Shelby American built this beast to test the marketability of the 427 Mustang, but gave up on the plan after the car sat unsold for a year, its $7,500 asking price scaring away potential buyers in droves.

Shelby American West Coast sales representative, who was responsible for promoting performance car sales at Mel Burns Ford in Long Beach, California, in 1967. No stranger to making Mustangs go fast, he was also the man responsible for Shelby's GT 350 drag car program, which produced 13 race-ready rockets—nine 1965s and four 1966s. In 1965 one of these "GT 350 Drag Mustang" packages produced an AHRA

quarter-mile record of 12.40 seconds at 113 miles per hour.

McCain simply couldn't resist the temptation to try building another special run of super Shelbys in 1967. A white 1967 GT 500, serial number 544, was chosen for the job, then transformed into the Super Snake at Shelby American's Los Angeles plant. This prototype was adorned with distinctive racing stripes (triple instead of

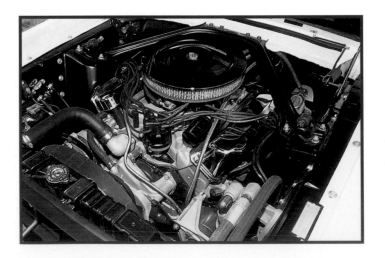

The *Super Snake*'s 427 big block was fitted with aluminum heads and a special "7,000-rpm kit." A big 780-cfm Holley supplied fuel/air and "bundle of snakes" headers hauled off spent gases. Output was reported at 520 horsepower.

double) and a revised grille to aid cooling. But all that was just icing on the cake.

The real story was the 427 that nestled nicely between the shock towers. Shelby's engineers just couldn't resist tinkering with it. A typical 427 medium-riser was impressive enough right out of the crate. Various tweaks here and there enhanced the attraction even further. For starters, the heads, single-carb intake, front cover, and water pump were made of weight-saving aluminum, as were the forged pistons. A special 7,000-rpm kit featuring a special valvetrain with exceptionally light valves, a beefier crank, and bulletproof rods. Additional high-rpm durability was guaranteed by a large-capacity oil pan and a remote oil filter and cooler.

Feeding this big bully was an enormous 780-cfm Holley four-barrel. At the other end of the process was a pair of racing-type "bundle of snakes" headers. Cam specs were apparently kept hush-hush, but results demonstrated that it too was a hotter item. The sum of all these parts equaled 520 horsepower on the dyno. That figure translated into 360 definitely usable horses in the real world.

Other Super Snake mechanicals came right off Ford parts shelves, save for the Traction-Master traction bars in back. A top-loader four-speed delivered all those ponies to a 4.11:1; Detroit Locker rear and front discs helped bring them all to a halt. The only other nonstock installation came at the corners with special Goodyear Thunderbolt tires.

To prove those tires' worth, the Shelby American team took the Super Snake to Goodyear's test facility in San Angelo, Texas. Various members of the press showed up as well, including *LIFE* magazine staffers and CBS television reporters. Carroll showed up some four hours after the car landed in San Angelo, but quickly made up for his tardiness by taking many of those left waiting for wild rides around Goodyear's high-banked 5-mile track. Then

The *Super Snake's* interior looks just as it did when Shelby used it for tire testing in 1967, right down to the fire extinguisher and full instrumentation (barely visible beneath the right-hand steering wheel spoke).

he left. As Shelby American chief engineer Fred Goodell remembered, Carroll handed him his helmet and said, "Freddy, I've got to go to Washington. You'll have to finish this. Just wear my helmet and nobody will know the difference." Goodell completed the test session, averaging 142 miles per hour for 500 miles. The Super Snake reportedly hit 170 miles per hour along the way.

As scintillating as those test results were, the Super Snake prototype didn't draw the attention McCain had hoped for. His original plan was to build 50 1967 427 Shelbys and sell them through Mel Burns Ford. But it was not to be. The Super Snake sat unsold on the lot for a year, its hefty $7,500 asking price scaring mere mortals away. Two airline pilots finally bought the car in 1968.

Various 427 GT 500s did make their way out of the Shelby American works in 1967. A production estimate of 50 circulated for years, but that undoubtedly was a reference to the number McCain initially intended to sell.

"No way there were 50," said Shelby American Automobile Club director Rick Kopec in 1991. "The number commonly associated with 427 GT 500s, 50 units, did come from the Super Snake. No matter what we try, that number clings to these cars." According to Fred Goodell, as many as 10 427 Shelbys were built in Los Angeles

in 1967. After sifting through half of Shelby American's invoices for that year, Kopec managed to find factory documentation for three of these high-flying GT 500s, including the Super Snake.

So where did the literally dozens of other 427 Shelbys come from? Private garage swaps produced some. And Mel Burns Ford wasn't the only dealership with a 427 GT 500 on the lot in 1967. Others, like Tasca Ford in East Providence, Rhode Island, also offered 427 retrofits. Determining how many of these "dealer-installed" cars (as opposed to the few factory-built examples) were sold is impossible, but Kopec guesses the number was small. His rationale involved cost.

"I don't think many dealers would've done an engine swap on a new Shelby," he said. "They were expensive enough as it was." A GT 500 cost $3,500 in 1967; a 427 in a crate, $2,000. You do the math.

There was another possible pipeline. "Once a buyer had his car and maybe blew the 428," continued Kopec, "it was easy to ask his dealer for it to be replaced with a 427, and he would pay the difference if the car was under warranty."

That's how so many 427 Shelbys came to be. As for the first, the Super Snake is alive and well in a Florida collector's hands. It still stands tall as perhaps the best of the breed.

Actually the 1966 changes were made in "running" fashion as the model year progressed. The first 252 1966 GT 350s built were actually 1965 "leftovers" still fitted with many of the previous year's features. Bare 15-inch rims remained standard for those 252 cars, as did the Koni shocks before they became a dealer-installed option. Fourteen-inch, five-spoke Magnum 500 wheels became standard with 1966 GT 350 number 253. The Cragar-supplied 15-inch five-spokes were optional for the early leftover models. Optional for later cars was a new 14-inch aluminum-alloy 10-spoke wheel.

Not all GT 350s in 1966 had back seats either. Reportedly as many as 82 of the 1965 leftovers were shipped to Shelby American as two-seaters, with some of these cars apparently being fitted with a rear seat as a dealer option. Another 1965 standard Shelby touch, the override traction arms with their welded-on brackets, continued in place until their supply ran out, apparently after about 800 1966 GT 350s were built. Traction-Master bolt-on traction bars were used from then on.

Another new option for 1966 was a Paxton supercharger that reportedly boosted horsepower by 46 percent compared to the normally aspirated Shelby 289. According to *Motor Trend*, the blower boost translated into a sizzling quarter-mile pass of 14.0 seconds at 102 miles per hour.

Overall a more socially acceptable machine, the second-edition GT 350 attracted nearly 2,400 buyers, including the Hertz Rent-A-Car company, which put 1,002 GT 350s into its fleet in 1966. All of these "GT 350H" models were fitted with Magnum 500 wheels, and most were painted black. Shelby American also created a GT 350 convertible in 1966, although all six built were not initially offered to the public. Instead they either stayed with Shelby or were given as gifts to valued "friends" of the company. These topless cars were the last six GT 350s off the line in 1966. Each was painted a different color: yellow, green, blue, red, white, or pink. All had under-dash air conditioners, and five of the six were automatics. They also featured nonfunctional side scoops because the top mechanism precluded the installation of the internal ductwork.

Another new model appeared in 1967 as the big-block GT 500. Various body modifications made both cars look less like Mustangs, more like Shelbys.

The GT 500 was replaced midyear in 1968 by the GT 500KR. "KR" stood for "king of the road," a claim backed up in spades by the new 428 Cobra Jet V-8. The 15-inch 10-spoke wheels were an option in 1968.

As it had since 1967, the Shelby interior in 1969 featured a padded roll bar with inertia-reel shoulder harnesses as standard equipment.

The Shelby Mustang took on an identity completely its own in 1969, thanks to the addition of a fiberglass nose that sprouted scoops as if they were going out of style. The hood alone featured five different openings—three to let air in, two to let it back out.

The 1969 GT 350's standard engine was a 290-horsepower 351 Windsor small block. Modifications included an aluminum high-rise intake and finned aluminum valve covers.

Above the grille, a fiberglass hood, stretched to meet the extended nose, incorporated a large, wide scoop with dual inlets. Beneath the GT 350's hood was the ever-present 289, still rated at 306 horsepower even though the Tri-Y headers were traded for cast-iron Ford Hi-Po exhaust manifolds. A standard oil pan was also used in place of the oversized Cobra unit.

Functional louvers were added on each side of the hood scoop when optional air conditioning was ordered in 1967. Also functional were the new rear quarter side scoops, which came in two pairs: lower scoops for brake cooling, upper for extracting bad interior air.

The new Shelby image received a bold exclamation point in back. Cougar sequential taillights and a fiber-glass deck lid incorporating a large ducktail spoiler were added. Fiberglass quarter panel extensions formed the spoiler's end caps, while a pop-open gas cap and a valance with cutouts for chrome exhaust tips completed the look. Without a doubt, no one would ever mistake a 1967 Shelby for just another Mustang.

Beneath the skin, the 1967 Shelby suspension was the Mustang's heavy-duty package with a thicker front stabilizer bar, adjustable Gabriel shock absorbers, and variable-rate front coils thrown in for good measure. The export brace was again added between the shock towers, but the Monte Carlo bar wasn't. Fifteen-inch steel rims wearing mag-style full wheel covers (bor-rowed from the Thunderbird parts bin) were standard. Optional on early 1967 Shelbys were 15x7 Kelsey-Hayes MagStar wheels. Cast-aluminum 10-spoke wheels became an option later in the run.

Adding a big block into the Shelby Mustang mix was only natural after Ford widened the pony car flanks in 1967. But while the garden-variety 1967 Mustang was fitted with the 390 V-8, the new GT 500 was armed with a 355-horsepower 428 big block topped by twin Holley four-barrels. Although underhood num-bers looked intimidating, the GT 500 was by no means a monster street machine. It was no quicker than the 1965 GT 350. Yet it represented a very happy medium between what the disappointing 390 Mustang had to offer and the original GT 350's rough-and-ready brand of performance. In *Car and Driver*'s words, the GT 500 was "a grown-up sports car for smooth touring. No more wham-bam, thank you ma'am, just a purring, well-controlled tiger."

The 428 Cobra Jet returned as the GT 500's power source in 1969. Notice the ram-air ductwork and the screens across the cooling outlets at the hood's trailing edge.

Thanks to an extended fiberglass nosepiece, the third-edition Shelby was 3 inches longer than the con-ventional 1967 Mustang. Recessed deep in this nosepiece was a grille sporting twin driving lights. These lights were mounted in two different positions, together in the middle or at opposite ends of the grille, depending on the state the car was originally delivered to. Statutes in some states requiring a minimum distance between headlights accounted for the variation.

Below the grille, a fiberglass valance incorporated a large cutout that not only supplied more cooling air to the radiator but also made for a more aggressive appearance.

Mexican businessman Eduardo Velasquez marketed his own brand of Shelby Mustang through Mexican Ford dealerships from 1967 to 1971. These were all notchback coupes powered by small blocks: 289s, 302s, and 351s. The GT 350 Shelby De Mexico shown here is one of only 306 built for 1969. Production was 169 in 1967 and 203 in 1968. *Tom Glatch*

The 1967 restyle for the Shelby Mustang also added a ducktail spoiler and sequential taillights. This fastback is a 1968 GT 500KR—production of this model was 933. Another 318 KR convertibles were also built for 1968. *Ford Motor Company*

GT 500s even outsold their small-block brothers in 1967 on the way toward a new Shelby Mustang production high. Total sales were up 35 percent to 3,223, with 2,050 of those being of the big-block variety. Shelby American also experimented with two GT 500 prototypes that year, one a "notchback" coupe, the other a convertible. These were the last California-built Shelby Mustangs, before production moved from Los Angeles to the A. O. Smith plant in Livonia, Michigan. Shelby's lease at the airport was up and Dearborn officials needed no other excuse to bring the GT 350/500 "into the fold." Although they did have another—there was no high-quality fiberglass source

in the L.A. area, but there was in Canada not far from Detroit—Ford 's agenda was to gain full control over the Shelby Mustang's future. Shelby was fed up with the deal by 1967 anyway. He had wanted to build race cars, but Ford wanted only racing imagery, with a car designed for the road.

The Michigan-built models were renamed Shelby Cobra GT 350 and Shelby Cobra GT 500 in 1968. This was also the year that a convertible was finally officially offered to the public. Styling changes were minor, the most noticeable being the addition of safety-conscious side marker lights and the substitution of larger 1965 Thunderbird sequential taillights in place of the

Shelby Mustangs were last offered in 1970, although these were actually 1969 leftovers dressed up with black hood stripes.

All GT 500s built after 1968 were powered by the 428 Cobra Jet, and the KR reference was dropped after its short run.

1967 Cougar units used the previous year. The standard simulated-mag wheel cover was also restyled.

The really big news for 1968 arrived midyear as Ford's new 428 Cobra Jet V-8 became the heart of the GT 500, replacing the dual-carb 428. Although its advertised output was lower, 335 horses compared to 355, the 428 CJ was much more of a prime mover compared to its forerunner. "It's big and strong and very highly tuned," claimed a *Car Life* review. "At 6000 rpm, the Cobra Jet will pull a semi-trailer up Pikes Peak." Maybe that's why Ford changed the name after the CJ appeared. The big-block Shelby then was no longer just a GT 500, it was a GT 500KR, with those extra letters standing for "King of the Road." GT 500KR quarter-mile performance registered in the mid-14-second range, which was truly great news, especially considering that GT 350 standard power in 1968 dropped down to 250 horses, these supplied by Ford's enlarged 302 Windsor small block.

Ford built 1,251 GT 500KR models in 1968—933 fastbacks and 318 convertibles. Before that came 1,542 GT 500s. Of that total, 1,140 were fastbacks and 402 were convertibles. The total GT 350 production that year was 1,657, with the breakdown being 1,253 fastbacks and 404 convertibles.

In 1969 the KR reference was dropped because all GT 500s were now Cobra Jets. Meanwhile, the GT 350 again traded engines, this time receiving the 351 Windsor small block rated at 290 horsepower.

Housing either engine, 351 or 428, was an all-new fiberglass nose that both heightened exclusivity and foretold a few of the new frontal impressions to come for the 1971 Mustang. "NACA ducts," designed by the National Advisory Committee for Aeronautics for high-speed jet aircraft, abounded on the 1969 'glass hood: two up front supplied cooling air to the engine compartment, two in back let the hot air escape, and one in the middle fed the engine's ram-air system. The fiberglass fenders incorporated brake-cooling ducts ahead of the front wheels, and another set of scoops directed cooling air to the rear brakes. Two types of rear scoops were used, depending on body style. Fastback scoops were inset up high, while convertible scoops protruded and were set lower to avoid contact with the top mechanism.

Plans to continue Shelby Mustang production into the 1970s were considered. But fortunately—especially so in the case of this 1968 Cobra concept machine—the legacy was allowed to end on a relative high note. *Ford Motor Company, photo courtesy of Automobile Quarterly*

A duck-tailed spoiler, continued through since 1967, again brought up the rear, with the 1965 Thunderbird taillights carried over from 1968. Totally new were the side-by-side aluminum exhaust outlets that exited through the center of the rear valance panel. A new five-spoke wheel was standard at the corners. No optional rims or wheel covers were offered in 1969; however, some early cars were apparently fitted with Magnum 500s after defects showed up in the new five-spokes. Standard rubber was E70x15 Wide Ovals, with a wider F60 tire offered at extra cost.

As dynamic as the 1969 GT 350/500 was in appearances, it still wasn't enough to keep the string alive. More image than action, the final-edition Shelby Mustang was an attractive car, but not in the fashion originally envisioned by its creator. As *Car and Driver*'s Brock Yates explained, "the original Shelby GT 350 was a fire-breather, it would accelerate, brake and corner with a nimbleness only a Corvette could match. The GT 350, 1969-style, is little more than a tough-looking Mustang Grande—a Thunderbird for Hell's Angels. Certainly not the car of Carroll Shelby's dreams."

Shelby himself finally went to Ford vice president John Naughton in the fall of 1969 and asked that the Shelby Mustang be discontinued. Not only was the car no longer the road rocket Shelby originally concocted, it was also competing with its own brethren, the Boss 302 and Boss 429. The situation looked to Shelby like a rob-Peter-to-pay-Paul arrangement. Naughton agreed, and the case was closed. But there still remained many cars left in the pipeline. About 3,200 GT 350s and 500s were built for 1969 before the axe fell, and nearly 790 of these were still hanging around as the model year came to a close. The decision was then made to simply update these 1969 leftovers with 1970 serial numbers. The cars were dressed up with chin spoilers and black hood stripes—the last changes to be made before the sun set on the Shelby Mustang.

Ending the story then and there was only right. After all, last call for the two Boss Mustangs was just around the corner. Despite the car's decline in performance over the years, many Ford fans still feel that the Shelby Mustang tale closed on a relatively high note.

CHAPTER 6

SNAKE BITE
Big-block Cobra Jets, 1968–1971

Henry Ford II couldn't have been riding any higher. It was the summer of 1966, and his multimillion-dollar racing program had finally produced the glorious moment he had been waiting for. A Ford-powered racer winning the Indy 500 in May 1965 didn't quite do the trick. When a trio of GT-40s rolled triumphantly together across the finish line at Le Mans a year later, they put Ford Motor Company on top of the world. Chrysler could kick all the ass it wanted on NASCAR speedways here at home. Ford now truly was an international racing power. No more challenges remained on this planet, not with Enzo Ferrari vanquished with a vengeance in France. Within a 24-hour span, Total Performance had been translated into total domination.

Not so fast. Sure, Ford's historic 1-2-3 "photo-finish" at the 1966 Quatre Heures du Mans was worth celebrating. It represented the first time an American factory team had garnered Le Mans laurels. And the many dozens of NASCAR victories scored back in the States since 1963 represented true testaments to just how competitive Ford-powered products had become. On the track, that is.

On the street it was an entirely different tale as the Ford faithful couldn't help noticing all those GTOs, SS 396 Chevelles, and Hemi Mopars quickly leaving them in the dust. As far as regular-production performance was concerned, 1966 was an awful year for Ford. Nineteen-sixty-seven wasn't much better. Discounting those purpose-built rarely seen 427 Fairlanes, Dearborn essentially had nothing to offer loyal customers desiring to keep up with the GM Joneses on Detroit's fast track. Hi-Po Mustangs, while a barrel of fun to drive, simply proved the age-old adage that there was no substitute for cubic inches. Early GTOs relied on 100 more cubes. Ford's Fairlane GT, introduced in 1966, was nice, but too

Above: The 428 Cobra Jet was a force to be reckoned with, even with the Thermactor smog controls. Ford engineers conservatively rated the CJ at 335 horsepower. Seat-of-the-pants responses said otherwise. *Steve Statham*

Opposite: Ford put the Mustang on the musclecar map in April 1968 with the introduction of the 428 Cobra Jet FE-series V-8. The CJ option was available for all three body styles: fastback, coupe, and convertible. And all 1968-1/2 Cobra Jet Mustangs were GTs.

A team of Cobra Jet Mustangs took the NHRA Winternationals by storm in February 1968. The all-star cast of CJ drivers that showed up at Pomona that year included Don Nicholson (Dyno Don), Hubert Platt, Gas Ronda, Al Joniec, and Jerry Harvey. *Ford Motor Company*

All Cobra Jet Mustangs in 1968 came with a functional ram-air hood standard. Ram-air became a CJ option in 1969. *Ford Motor Company*

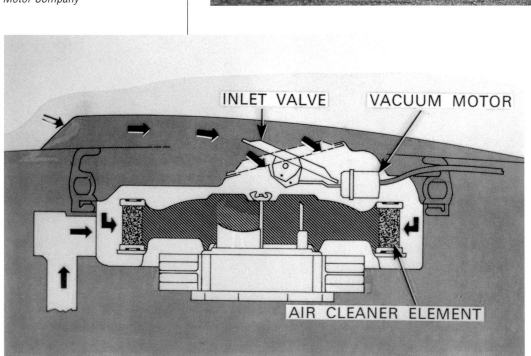

nice. It just couldn't stand up to all those big-block bullies then kicking up tons of sand on muscle beach.

A ray of hope did begin to shine in 1967 when the Mustang's engine bay was enlarged to make room for the original pony car's first big block, the venerable 390-ci FE-series V-8. The optional 390 GT V-8 was advertised at 320 horsepower, an impressive number that promised to win respect. That promise proved false, however. As *Car Life*'s curbside critics put it, "perhaps this superburger, if it is to be a superburger, needs a little more mustard."

What was a horsepower-hungry Ford customer to do? The answer was, wait a year. On April 1, 1968, Dearborn introduced its street performance savior, a car that propelled Ford's go-fast reputation to the forefront of the musclecar scene.

Inspiration for the 428 Cobra Jet came not from within, but from Rhode Island, with a little help from

Commonly reported production figures for the 1968-1/2 Cobra Jet Mustang put fastback totals at 2,253. The total run for all three bodies was 2,827.

Rarest of the CJ breed in 1968 was the convertible, of which maybe 10 were built. Coupe production was 564. *Steve Statham*

a fast-thinking automotive journalist working clean across the country in California.

Robert F. Tasca Sr.—Bob to most, the "Bopper" to many—became America's most successful Ford dealer in the 1960s. Founded in November 1953 at 777 Taunton Avenue in East Providence, Rhode Island, Tasca Ford had grown so fast that Dearborn officials began asking Bob how such a relatively small dealership could sell so many cars. Tasca kept no secrets and was soon advising other dealers, as well as Ford's executive elite, on how the game should be played. His corporate ties quickly reached all the way to the top, even to Henry II's office. When Bob Tasca talked, Ford listened.

By the mid-1960s, Tasca Ford reached the top of Ford's national sales rankings, and at the same time became the East Coast mecca for seekers of true Blue Oval performance. The two results were no coincidence.

If it was hot, it was there on Tasca's lot, per the Bopper's exacting plan. Bob Tasca has always known a good thing when he saw it. He has also always been able to sell cars like nobody's business. In the 1960s, peddling performance was the quickest way to sales success.

Late in 1961, Tasca organized a special high-performance division and made Dean Gregson its manager. The dealership then began sponsoring its first drag car early the next year. Tasca Ford put together its own race team late in 1962, with Bill Lawton doing the driving. Two years later, Lawton piloted Tasca Ford's 427 Thunderbolt to a Super Stock championship at the NHRA Winternationals, followed by an A/FX title in a Holman-Moody SOHC Mustang in 1965. By then "win on Sunday, sell on Monday" had become one of Tasca's prime mottoes. As long as Fords were winners, so too was Bob Tasca's dealership. But there was a flip side.

As Tasca told *Super Stock* magazine in 1968, "we did well from 1963 to 1965, when the car-buying market was a young one. [Then] younger people [became] disenchanted with Ford's performance on the street and stopped buying. Consequently, we had to cut back the racing budget that year." Dearborn's dwindling presence in the musclecar market left Tasca distraught. Detroit reportedly sold 634,434 high-performance cars (classed as those powered by at least 300 horses) in 1966. Ford's share of that pie was a paltry 7.5 percent—"shameful for a 'Total Performance' company," claimed Bob Tasca in a 1967 *Hot Rod* report.

Equally shameful, at least from a Tasca Ford point of view, was Ford's response to the situation. New big-block Mustangs had barely begun rolling off delivery trucks in the fall of 1966 when the Tasca crew discovered that bigger definitely didn't mean better. As Dean Gregson told *Hot Rod* in late 1967, "We sold a lot of 390 Mustangs last fall and into the winter, but by March they dropped off to practically nothing. That's when the snow melted off the asphalt." On dry land, the big-block pony car was no match for its GM rivals. "We found the car so non-competitive, we began to feel we were cheating the customer," continued Gregson. "He was paying for what he saw advertised in all the magazines as a fast car, but that was not what he was getting. So we did something about it."

Tasca Ford's solution actually came about by accident. Literally. While doing a little "street testing" one night after work, a Tasca man over-revved the 390 in a gold 1967 Mustang GT coupe. Instead of simply replacing the blown FE, Gregson's team chose a clean slate, starting with a 428 Police Interceptor short block. A GTA 390 hydraulic cam was stuffed inside and reworked 1963-1/2 low-riser 427 heads featuring enlarged exhaust ports went on top of the block. A big 735-cfm Holley four-barrel carb finished things off. The result was a basically "stock" big-block Mustang, built up only with available Ford parts, that was able to turn the quarter-mile in a startling 13.39 seconds at 105 miles per hour.

Tasca Ford had clearly proved what some simple mixing and matching of existing hardware could do for Dearborn's performance image, and the dealership did so more than once, building various 428 Mustangs in 1967. With news of the powerhouse Mustang beginning

to circulate, *Hot Rod* magazine sent technical editor Eric Dahlquist to check out what Bob Tasca had wrought. He witnessed the awesome performance of Tasca's KR-8 Mustang—*KR* for King of the Road, 8 for 1968.

Tasca knew how easy it would be for Ford to re-create his KR-8 Mustang on the regular production line. Dahlquist recognized this plain truth too, and he decided to give the company a little push. He constructed the lead page of his November 1967 Tasca Mustang *HRM* feature as a ballot. The headline read, "Ford's Ultimate Super Cars." Above that were two boxes marked "YES" and "NO." He then asked readers to vote on whether Ford should produce the 428 Mustang he described. He told readers to "circle your choice in the box provided and return to: Mr. Henry Ford II, Dearborn, Michigan 48121."

"The only way to get attention was to let Henry Ford II himself receive the responses, and boy did he get 'em," chuckled Dahlquist. *HRM* pages marked yes soon began piling up on Henry's desk. As Dahlquist recalled, "It wasn't long before a Ford public relations person was calling me asking that I 'turn off the spigot.' 'Enough already, we are going to build it.'"

Dahlquist's efforts alone did not open the door to the Cobra Jet's creation, although they certainly didn't hurt. "The next time I went back to Ford [after the *HRM* article ran] I got a nice reception," he said. "The engineers were very happy."

Cobra Jet Mustangs were naturals at the track, where things like radios and heaters are rarely needed. Notice the plate across the space where the deleted radio on this 1968-1/2 CJ fastback would've resided.

Ram-air became an option for the 428 Cobra Jet in 1969. And this wasn't just any garden-variety ram-air system, it was the glorious poke-right-through-the-hood Shaker.

Among them was Bill Barr, then principal design engineer in charge of FE-series V-8 design and testing. According to him it was Tasca who basically kicked in the doors. "Bob likes to say he was the father of the Cobra Jet, and he's right," said Barr. "When Tasca came to town, he was always immediately given an audience, and this time he flogged the company for what he wanted. He railed for the Cobra Jet. He supplied the notice and political pressure to get this thing going, and that prompted us to do something like he had done."

Barr's team V-8 began with a beefed-up passenger-car 428 block recast in nodular iron alloy with thickened main bearing bulkheads and extra reinforcing ribbing. Typical two-bolt main bearing caps were retained to keep things simple and cost-effective. As it was, engineers pegged this new engine's operating rev range at about a 1,000 rpm less than the high-winding, 6,500-revolution 427s, they with their battleship-tough, cross-bolted, four-bolt lower end. In the 428's case, two bolts would be enough to hold things together. Lower-end durability was also enhanced by a nodular-iron crankshaft and burly Police Interceptor connecting rods with

odd-sized 13/32-inch bolts. Pistons were cast-aluminum flat-tops. Compression was 10.6:1.

Key to the combination was the addition of 427 cylinder heads, also specially prepared for this application. These heads were drilled for emissions-control plumbing and machined to accept two different exhaust manifold bolt patterns—each exhaust port face had four holes instead of two. Existing 427 FE manifolds used an over/under bolt pattern; those cast for the 1968 light-car application featured a side-by-side pattern. These heads also featured bigger ports and valves (2.09-inch intakes, 1.66 exhausts) compared to standard 428 units.

Additional CJ components included a cast-iron copy of the aluminum PI intake manifold and free-flowing cast-iron exhaust manifolds. The 390 GT hydraulic cam spec'ed out at 270/290 (intake/exhaust) degrees duration and 0.481/0.490 inch of lift. While the 427 and Carroll Shelby's GT 500 428 of 1967 both used dual carbs, the 428 CJ relied on a single Holley four-barrel, albeit a big one at 735 cfm. By 1968 large four-barrels had already superseded the dual-carb setups used earlier in the 1960s atop top-performance

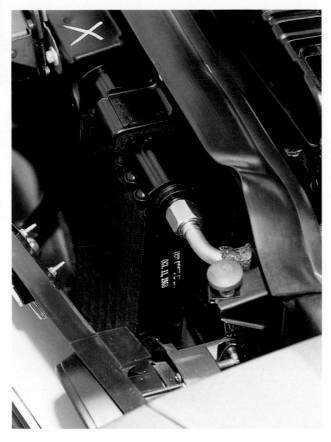

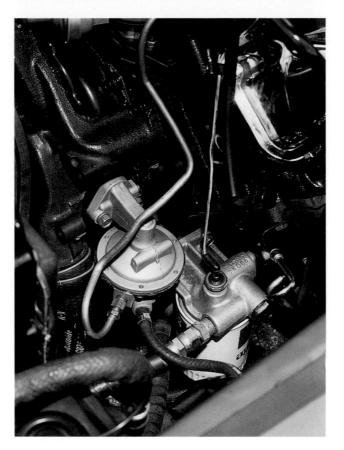

Mustang buyers in 1969 were also treated to the Super Cobra Jet 428 which, among other things, included an external oil cooler located on the front of the radiator core support on the driver side.

The 428 SCJ used a special oil filter mount that routed the lubricant to the cooler and back again.

engines. As Barr explained, "We could've, of course, put on more carburetor, but we had enough power already. Besides, drivers on the street were limited by only so much ability to put all that power on the ground."

Advertised 428 CJ output was 335 horsepower at 5,600 rpm. Maximum torque was 445 ft-lb at 3,400 revs. Optional ram-air equipment (for midsized Ford and Mercury applications) didn't change that output figure because, as Barr pointed out, dyno testing was done in a static situation that couldn't utilize forced induction.

Federally mandated emissions equipment, however, was forced upon this new big block. Ford's Thermactor air pump was standard. Many performance customers may have complained about this apparent nuisance in 1968, but Barr's men "weren't overly concerned": "The Thermactor didn't make that big of a difference in performance. It was not as sophisticated a design as you might think, and it did of course induce slightly more back pressure in the exhaust manifold at the exhaust valve, but I don't believe it even made as much as a 5 horsepower difference," Barr said.

Ford offered the 428 Cobra Jet as a midyear "1968-1/2" option for Fairlanes, Torinos, Cougars,

and midsized Mercurys, but the CJ garnered the most attention as the brave new heart of a new, truly muscular Mustang. CJ Mustang production commenced at the Dearborn assembly plant on December 13, 1967. First came at least 50 specially prepared fastbacks: lightweight, strip-ready super-stock Mustangs with all sealers and sound deadeners deleted. These models, all painted Wimbledon White, were built for one job: to promote Ford's newest breed of pony car performance at the drags.

Regular production of street-going CJ Mustangs began after the run of super-stock drag cars was completed. Dealers received notice of the 428 Cobra Jet engine option on March 29, 1968. Priced at $420, this powerful package was offered in all three body styles: fastback, coupe, and convertible. The first was the most popular choice by far. Latest reports put 1968-1/2 Cobra Jet Mustang production at 2,827. Of that total, 2,253 were fastbacks, 564 were coupes, and 10 were convertibles.

All "standard" Mustang Cobra Jets built in 1968 featured a functional ram-induction hood with distinctive black striping. The white super-stock models did

When Tasca Speaks...

Robert F. Tasca Sr.'s half century career in the automobile business began in May 1943 when he went to work as a 17-year-old grease monkey for Sandager Ford in Cranston, Rhode Island. It wasn't long before he began climbing the company ladder, educating himself in mechanics and marketing along the way. He rose to sales manager in 1948, then manager the following year. Five years later Tasca left Sandager and opened his own dealership on Taunton Avenue in East Providence.

Curious Ford officials first came to Rhode Island in 1958 to see for themselves how such a small dealership could be selling so many Fords—the most in New England. "We were highly successful, and they wanted to know why we were and how we did it," remembered Tasca. "I was never in fear of letting the world know how we did it. I never had any secrets. I've always shared my information."

That he did, both with other dealers and Ford Motor Company execs. His ties in Dearborn soon ran right to the top as he took on what essentially was a nonpaying consulting role. Bunkie Knudsen often turned to Tasca as an advisor during his short stay atop Ford in 1968 and 1969. Knudsen valued performance as a selling point, and Tasca was then selling performance like there was no tomorrow. Helping promote those sales was Tasca Ford's national championship drag-racing team. "If you win on Sunday at the drags, you'll sell on Monday on the showroom," he told *Super Stock* magazine in 1968. "Win on Sunday, sell on Monday" was one of Bob Tasca's prime mottoes throughout the 1960s.

Knudsen too recognized that speed sells, but Bunkie moved too fast for Ford. "I didn't give him long," said Tasca. "He wasn't Ford's style of management, and he wasn't Iacocca's type. You had two guys who wanted to be the leader. Something had to give."

Tasca continued advising Lee Iacocca after he gained the president's post in December 1970 following Knudsen's firing. He also had Donald Petersen's ear after he became chief in 1980. When the Bopper had an audience, he never failed to speak his mind. If he thought there was something wrong with Ford's products, he said so. Often. "Iacocca once told me, 'why don't you open Tasca Motor Company?'" recalled Bob Sr. in 1992. "'Nothing we build is good enough for you.'" That, of course, wasn't true. Tasca

Ford General Manager Donald Frey admires the silver bowl awarded to Bob Tasca (right) by *American Rodding* magazine in honor of Tasca's 505 Mustang (foreground), a customized 1965 2+2 that *American Rodding* called "America's Perfect Performance Car." *Ford Motor Company, photo courtesy of* Automobile Quarterly

simply wanted the cars he sold to be the best they could be. "On my tombstone someday I hope to have it say, 'he helped Ford go from good to great,'" he said.

Bob Tasca reportedly could have helped even more. Between 1958 and 1963, he turned down three opportunities to join Ford Motor Company full time. Intensely loyal to his wife and children, Tasca chose to concentrate on keeping his family, and the family business, together in Rhode Island. "I could have gone high in Dearborn," he said. "But I wouldn't trade my accomplishments here for anything, not even the chairmanship of Ford."

What he did do was agree to use his business as a "training dealership" to help instruct other Ford Motor Company dealers worldwide. At one point, Tasca was overseeing at least one sales seminar a month at locations across this country, as well as throughout Europe. "In 30 years I've trained thousands of dealers," he said. The most important lesson he teaches always

Robert F. Tasca, Sr. (far left) poses in front of his East Providence, Rhode Island, dealership in 1967. To his right is a street-going GT-40 Mk III, and next to it is the Mustang coupe that became the "prototype" for the 428 Cobra Jet. *Courtesy Robert F. Tasca, Sr.*

Bill Lawton drove this A/FX Mustang for Tasca Ford's drag-race team in 1965. Lawton won back-to-back Winternational championships, first in a Tasca Thunderbolt in 1964, then in this Mustang in 1965. *Courtesy Robert F. Tasca, Sr.*

involves giving customers what they want—quality cars and top-notch service. As one service department employee said in 1992, "Bob Tasca will do whatever it takes, whatever the cost to satisfy a customer. He will not quit until that guy leaves here happy."

Times have changed, as has the market, yet Tasca's success has never waned. Factory performance died in the early 1970s, as did Tasca Ford's drag-race team. But Bob Tasca simply shifted gears. In October 1971, at Iacocca's request, the Bopper traded Fords for Lincolns and Mercurys and moved his business about a mile east down Taunton Avenue into Seekonk, Massachusetts. There, Tasca Lincoln-Mercury was soon thriving and, by 1986, was the world's leading L-M dealership.

One month after Mustang collectors marked the Cobra Jet's 25th birthday in 1993, Robert F. Tasca Sr., was honored for his 50 uninterrupted years working with Ford Motor Company. Although officially retired, the elder Tasca still stands close by while sons Bob Jr., Carl, and David run the family business.

Make that businesses. In 1994, Fournier Ford, the dealership that had taken Tasca Ford's place at 777 Taunton Avenue, closed up shop and sold the building back to the Tascas. The family then reopened Tasca Ford at its old location in October that year. In December, more than 10,000 people came to see Tasca Ford's grand re-opening. Even Tasca Ford's old 1964 Thunderbolt NHRA champion race car returned to the front window to entice onlookers inside the showroom once more.

With two highly successful dealerships now operating, Bob Tasca is understandably proud of his achievements, as well as his family's. Yet he remains humble. "Without Ford Motor Company people's talents, I couldn't have achieved what I did," he said. "Bob Tasca was not a smart man. Bob Tasca learned from a lot of very, very smart people at Ford, basically because I asked a lot of questions and remembered most of the answers. The Ford-Tasca partnership has been one that I cherish."

Ford, Lincoln, and Mercury buyers still benefit from that partnership.

Tasca Ford's racing efforts quickly escalated in the 1960s as injected 427 SOHC engines and funny car bodies replaced the factory superstocks. The *Mystery 9* name referred to the car's ability to run the quarter-mile in nine seconds. *Courtesy Robert F. Tasca, Sr.*

not get the hood stripe. CJ customers were also required to check off a host of extras, including the GT equipment group (again, the lightweight drag cars were not GTs), which added a heavy-duty suspension, styled-steel wheels wearing F70 rubber, C-stripes, fog lamps, chrome exhaust tips, and GT identification. Also on the list of mandatory options were power front disc brakes, braced shock towers, an 8,000-rpm tach (standard with a four-speed, optional with the C6 automatic), a beefy 9-inch rear end (with 3.50:1 gears; 3.91:1 and 4.30:1 ratios were also available) featuring rugged 31-spline axles, and staggered rear shocks (for four-speed models only). The typical bottom line for a 1968-1/2 CJ Mustang was about $3,700. Base price for a garden-variety fastback that year was $2,689. Most agreed the grand or so premium for Cobra Jet power was well worth it.

As for the CJ name, no one is really sure who deserves credit, although it's obvious where the Cobra theme originated. According to Bob Tasca, Lee Iacocca had paid a high price for the rights to Shelby's sneaky snake label and wasn't about to see all that cash go to waste, which left Tasca's KR suggestion out of the running. The Bopper's King of the Road tag did, however, find a home on the CJ-powered 1968 GT 500 Shelby Mustang.

"We already had the snake idea in our heads," echoed Bill Barr. "And we didn't do this like we normally did. We didn't just roll out the product with everyone standing around it scratching their asses trying to name it. The idea was already rolling by that stage. Some artist in Styling had already created a drawing of the Cobra emblem—the snake with the wheels and exhausts coming out of its tale. We had the drawing, then the name came from there." Some might infer that the Cobra Jet moniker was perhaps a knock-off of Chevy's "Turbo-Jet" V-8 references. Barr doesn't agree. "The sales guys didn't necessarily try to one-up Chevrolet," he said. "They just might have misinterpreted that drawing, thinking those exhausts in back were jets."

Witnesses who first experienced Cobra Jet performance probably saw it similarly. "We'd been testing a lot of cars," said Dahlquist, "and Fords had been way at the back of the pack. Then this Mustang shows up and it's a rocket ship. Ford from last to first in one jump." Added Barr, "the Cobra Jet was so strong we had a hard time keeping the tires on the road. So we put our engine in that little car and adjusted the chassis. We could drive around all day in fourth gear—from 10 miles per hour to 100 in fourth—because it was such a strong engine."

Interestingly, it was also somewhat of a softy in everyday operation. Explained Barr, "the early 427s and Hi-Po 289s could be hard to start and didn't idle very well. The Cobra Jet was much better; it was as good or better than the 390 GT, which was a very streetable engine. And it was considerably better than [Chrysler's] Hemi; it was much more docile and streetable. But once you went down on the loud pedal, this baby could really fly. On the street, the Cobra Jet was absolutely awesome. Nothing I saw anywhere could touch it. For stoplight Grand Prixes the 428 Cobra Jet was the bee's knees because nothing could stay with it."

In Tasca's opinion, "the Cobra Jet [Mustang] began the era of Ford's supremacy in performance. It was the fastest, in my opinion, the fastest production car built in the world at that point, and I'm not talking top speed. I'm talking run fast, get up and go. It was a 12-second street machine."

Barr's engineering tests of a box-stock Cobra Jet Mustang pilot car put quarter-mile performance at 13.4 seconds. According to him, all CJ Mustangs sold in 1968 were potentially that quick. "When we saw the magazine test scores of about a 13.6, we figured they must have had a poor driver."

The results Barr referred to were published in *Hot Rod*'s March 1968 issue by Dahlquist, who had pressed Dearborn for a first look at a Cobra Jet in exchange for "turning off the spigot." Many have since written that the Mustang Dahlquist received was a specially prepared model, perhaps even tweaked by Bill Stroppe's shop. But Dahlquist claimed such shenanigans weren't possible given the time element involved. "I believe it couldn't have been a Stroppe-built car. It showed up from Dearborn with only 3 or 4 miles on the odometer when it rolled off the truck. My boss, Ray Brock, said 'Eric, you're going to have to put some miles on that car, you can't test it like that. Sorry to ruin your weekend.' On top of that, Stroppe would've needed a week or two with the car. It showed up too quick for that."

If anything, the car was probably one of those first 50 super stock specials. Dahlquist does remember it lacking sealer and sound deadener. He also remembers it turning a sizzling 13.56-second elapsed-time once it was broken in, performance that inspired his now-famous conclusion: "The CJ will be the utter delight of every Ford lover and the bane of all the rest because, quite frankly, it is probably the fastest regular production sedan ever built." Dahlquist's words, in turn, inspired Ford promotional people to quote his *Hot Rod* review in their Cobra Jet ads. But rascals as they were, Dearborn's admen substituted ". . . is the fasted running Pure Stock in the history of man," a line used separately near the end of Dahlquist's article, in place of the correct ending of the quote.

From there the Cobra Jet Mustangs rolled rapidly into history, taking the 1968 Winternationals by storm as a wave of white CJ fastbacks driven by Al Joniec, Dyno Don Nicholson, Hubert Platt, and the boys dominated the Super Stock field. Joniec's Cobra Jet took top S/S honors at Pomona that year with a run of 12.12 seconds at 109.48 miles per hour. A *Car Craft* track test of a super-stock Mustang CJ, driven by Dyno

Don and Platt, pushed the envelope even further to 11.62 seconds at 119.7 miles per hour. To that *Car Craft* managing editor John Raffa wrote that "Ford's new 428 Cobra Jet Mustang Super/Stocker can best be described as a car with hair!"

The hairy Cobra Jet returned in 1969 as standard equipment beneath the hood of the Fairlane Cobra. It was optional on all other Fairlanes, and the same went for the Mustang, be it a GT, Mach 1, Grande, or plain-Jane SportsRoof, coupe or convertible. The GT options group was no longer a required option. Nor was ram-air equipment automatically included in the 428 Cobra Jet V-8 deal, now priced at $287. The basic CJ big block in 1969 came topped with a conventional single-snorkel air cleaner fitted with a vacuum-operated "pop-off valve" that sprung open at full throttle to allow more underhood air pressure into the Holley carb below. The unit was topped with a chrome-plated lid. The stamped-steel valve covers were also chromed, as they had been the previous year.

The deletion of ram-air from the standard Cobra Jet package in 1969 didn't change the advertised output

It was the 429 Cobra Jet's free-breathing heads that precluded its use as a Mustang option before 1971. This 385-series big block was wider than its FE-series Cobra Jet forerunner. It couldn't fit between Mustang fenders until Bunkie Knudsen's enlarged body debuted for 1971. *Ford Motor Company*

figure: It remained at 335 horsepower. Putting ram-air, now an option, back atop the 428 CJ didn't change anything either: 335 horsepower again. Adding optional ram-air also produced another familiar figure—$420, the same price asked for the force-fed 428 Cobra Jet in 1968. While the base 428 CJ was apparently available for the luxury-conscious Grande, Ford paperwork was explicit concerning the hissing, hairy Shaker—"N/A with Grande" read the last line of the ram-air 428 Cobra Jet engine option entry in 1969.

The one thing that did increase in 1969 was the ram-air CJ's image. The ram-air hood used in 1968 looked like so many other sporty hoods found on so many other sporty rivals of the day. Beneath the 1968-1/2 CJ Mustang's typically scooped hood was an air cleaner that sealed to the hood's underside to allow cooler, denser ambient air a quick passage from the functional scoop above into that hungry Holley's four throats. In 1969 that conventional scoop was traded for the legendary "Shaker," which attached directly to the top of the air cleaner and protruded up through an opening in the hood. When the Cobra Jet started shaking side to side under torque load, so too did this ribbed, black scoop—thus the formal name. The "hey-look-at-me" Shaker easily ranked as the coolest hood scoop to date out of Detroit.

The sinister black Shaker was also fully functional, as a vacuum-controlled bypass flap inside automatically opened wide whenever the pedal met the metal, allowing outside air to ram (ram-air, get it?) into the four waiting venturis with far less restriction than that found during typical operation. Normally, the ram-air 428 CJ sucked in heated underhood atmosphere through the air cleaner's conventional snorkel. According to factory paperwork, ram-air Cobra Jets were also dressed up with finned cast-aluminum valve covers, but apparently not every Shaker-equipped CJ received these attractive pieces.

Ford officials once more chose not to adjust advertised CJ output when the Shaker scoop was in place. Both 428s, ram-air or not, still carried 335-horse ratings in 1969. Informed witnesses knew better. When *Car and Driver*'s leadfoots tested a 1969 428 Cobra Jet Mach 1, they taped the Shaker's opening shut and instantly recorded quarter-mile elapsed times that were 0.2 seconds and 2 miles per hour slower than those put down by the free-breathing CJ. "Ford can be justifiably proud," read *Car and Driver*'s conclusions concerning the Shaker. "It works."

Ford engineers were also proud of another optional addition to the CJ performance package. A 428 Cobra Jet became a Super Cobra Jet whenever a buyer checked off the "Drag Pack" rear axle option. The Drag Pack option consisted of either a 3.91:1 or 4.30:1 strip-ready axle ratio in a Traction-Lok limited-slip differential. Recognizing that these gears were best suited for on-track action, the engineering team further built up the CJ into the SCJ by adding tougher forged aluminum pistons (in place of the CJ's cast slugs) and beefy "LeMans" rods. Developed for Ford's GT-40 427, these super-strong connecting rods were held onto the crank by cap screws and larger 7/16-inch rod bolts instead of conventional nuts and the Cobra Jet's standard 13/32-inch bolts. Adding these heavier rods and pistons, of course, required rebalancing the engine. To do this, an external counter-balancer (among other things) was incorporated behind the crank's vibration damper.

A racing-style external oil cooler, which was mounted on the front of the radiator core support on the driver side, completed the Super Cobra Jet package. Some reports claimed that all 428 SCJs, like the ram-air Cobra Jets, also featured finned aluminum valve covers. But those dress-up pieces were reportedly introduced on January 14, 1969, apparently meaning that any Super Cobra Jets (or Shaker-equipped CJs) built before that date had the typical chromed stamped-steel covers. Whatever the case, it is not correct to assume that the presence of the steel covers automatically rules out the presence of a Super Cobra Jet. Some have bright steel, and some have the dull aluminum.

The 428 Cobra Jet remained a strong street performance option through 1970 but only for Ford Motor Company's pony cars, the Mustang, and its Cougar cousin. Production of 428 Cobra Jet and Super Cobra Mustangs for 1969 and 1970 was 13,193 and 2,671, respectively, bringing the total three-year run to 18,691 before Ford finally ended the long-in-the-tooth FE-series big-block run. A notable SCJ change in 1970 involved the arrival of the gnarly, no-spin Detroit Locker differential, which became part of the Drag Pack option along with the 4.30:1 ratio. The Traction-Lok remained for the 3.91:1 ratio.

From 1969 on, Cobra Jet Mustangs came in all forms, from supersporty Mach 1s to plain-Jane notchback coupes. This 1971 coupe features a nonfunctional "NASA" hood, but beneath that bonnet is a very virile 429 Cobra Jet.

Ford's new, cleaner-running 385-series Cobra Jet, the 429, superseded its 428 FE forerunner in other 1970 models, including the hot Torino Cobra. Even though he also contributed to the second-edition CJ, Bill Barr wasn't necessarily convinced that progress in this case was an entirely good thing. In in-house tests, "a 429 Cobra Jet never beat a 428 Cobra Jet," he said. Barr also claims "probably nothing" in his 35-year career at Ford could quite compare to what he achieved in the heady days of the 1960s, when engineers were still free to design engines to run and Cobras could be jets: "From 1962 to '70, it was nonstop fun, more fun than people should be allowed."

All the fun didn't exactly stop in 1970, although it was clear by then that those who preferred life in the fast lane better get it while the gettin' was good. Federal emissions standards were seemingly growing tougher by the day. This factor alone would have been enough to strangle the life out of musclecars like the Cobra Jet Mustangs. Add to that the higher and higher costs of insuring these beasts, coupled with all the attention being given to automotive safety issues at that time, and anyone with eyes could see what lay ahead. Drastically lowered compression in nearly all of Detroit's 1971 engines—this done in preparation for the upcoming mandated use of catalytic converters—served as a wake-up call to any horsepower hound who had yet to get the message. By the end of the year, all the great big-block performance powerplants—426 Hemi and triple-carb 440 Mopars, LS-6 454 Chevy, and, yes, Cobra Jet Ford—would be dead and buried.

But at least Ford engineers were allowed to keep the Cobra Jet legacy running, however briefly, before the nails hit the coffin. Mustang buyers, who in 1970 had watched as the new Torino Cobra beat nearly everything in sight, woke up one year later to find the Cobra's 429 CJ V-8 on the pony car options list, this thanks to the 1971 restyled, enlarged body. Like the 428 CJ in 1969 and 1970, the 429 Cobra Jet was available for all 1971 models, save for the exclusively powered Boss 351 Mustang. The extra charge for the 429 Cobra Jet was $372; $436 for the CJ-R—*R* for ram-air, of course.

Ram-air Mustangs in 1971 were fitted with yet another new hood, this one featuring two scoops up near the leading edge. Ford promotional people "erroneously" called this a "NASA hood," undoubtedly

This 1971 coupe was clearly set up for racing when originally purchased. No radio and no frills, just a 429 Cobra Jet, heavy-duty suspension and dog-dish hubcaps. Those plain 15x7 steel wheels were required whenever the F60 tires were added. In most cases, however, buyers opted for the flashy Magnum 500 wheel instead of the mundane rim.

Advertised output for the 429 Cobra Jet without ram-air was 370 horsepower. Trading this chrome-topped air cleaner for the unit that sealed to the fully functional "NASA" hood upped the CJ output ante in 1971 to 375 horses.

because they figured many more Americans would relate to the National Aeronautics and Space Administration than its predecessor, the National Advisory Committee for Aeronautics. One of NACA's innovations was the aptly named "NACA duct," an air inlet specially designed to maximize flow in high-speed situations—say, like flying at the speed of sound. Once discovered by race car builders in the 1960s, NACA ducts began showing up in all locations where brakes (and drivers) needed cooling and hoods needed scooping. NACA was long-since forgotten by the time those two NACA-style scoops were added to the Mach 1 hood in 1971. On the flip side, practically every human on this planet, and certainly all those on the moon, knew what NASA was. Realizing this, Ford's label-makers transformed the NACA scoop into the NASA scoop.

All that aside, the twin NACA ducts on the 1971 NASA hood funneled cooler air into a plastic housing on the hood's underside. This housing, in turn, was sealed to the air cleaner by a large rubber "doughnut" similar to the arrangement used atop the 1968-1/2 428 Cobra Jet. Vacuum-controlled diaphragms inside the plastic ductwork opened up at full throttle to allow denser outside air to flow directly to the air cleaner,

which again used a conventional snorkel to breathe in underhood air during normal operation.

And again, engineers chose not to play with output numbers. With or without ram-air, the 429 Cobra Jet was advertised at 370 horsepower, only 10 ponies more than the mundane 429 Thunder Jet passenger-car big block it was based on. Right. The improvements made to transform Thunder to Cobra undoubtedly were worth more than that, but the idea was to fool the insurance cops.

Engineers took the relatively tame Thunder Jet and added a 715-cfm Rochester Quadra-Jet four-barrel on a cast-iron dual-plane intake for starters. Perhaps the best-breathing street heads ever bolted on a Ford V-8 were also added. These CJ cylinder heads featured huge, rounded intake ports. Exhaust passages were also enormous, as were valves: 2.242-inch intakes, 1.722-inch exhausts. Bumping those staggered valves was a potent hydraulic long-duration (282-degree intake, 296-degree exhaust) cam. Lift was a hefty 0.506 inch for both valves. Compression was 11.3:1. Unlike the 428 Cobra Jet, the 429 CJ block was held together on the bottom end by four-bolt main bearing caps, but only for the three inner crankshaft journals. Front and rear mains were two-bolt

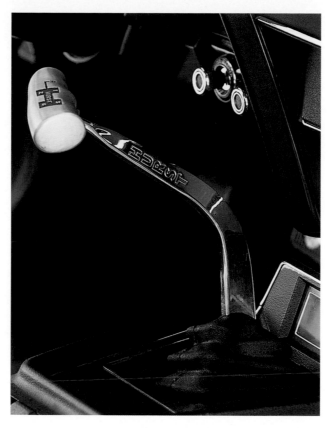

units. A rev limiter also helped keep the reciprocating mass in place.

A close-ratio top-loader four-speed or heavy-duty Cruise-O-Matic C6 automatic transmission went behind the 429 Cobra Jet. Mandatory options included power front discs, the competition suspension, and F70 tires. Then, of course, there was the ever-present Drag Pack. For 1971 this option included a choice between the 3.91:1 Traction-Lok differential and the 4.11:1 Detroit Locker. The price was $155 for the former, $207 for the latter.

Choosing the Drag Pack transformed the Cobra Jet into a Super Cobra Jet. But this time the transformation was quite a bit more dramatic. Inside, heavy-duty forged aluminum pistons were stuffed into the 429 SCJ's block, as was a more potent solid-lifter cam with 300-degrees of duration and a 0.509-inch lift. On top, the Cobra Jet's Q-Jet carb was replaced by a larger 780-cfm Holley four-barrel bolted to a specially machined cast-iron intake. An external oil cooler was again included as part of the Super Cobra Jet deal. Not all 429 SCJ Mustangs were fitted with this cooler, however, including apparently most of the cars driven by 4.11 gears. Go figure.

Just as Bill Barr said, track tests of the heavier 1971 429 Cobra Jet Mustang never produced results like those that Eric Dahlquist enthusiastically reported for the 428 CJ in *Hot Rod* in 1968. *Sports Car Graphic*'s editors couldn't say enough of how the nose-heavy, far-from-agile 429 Mustang failed to excite them, but they didn't call themselves *SPORTS CAR Graphic* for nothing. *SCG*'s October 1970 issue reported a quarter-mile run of 14.6 seconds, topping out at 99.4 miles per hour. More representative of the 429 CJ Mustang's true straight-line potential was a February 1971 *Super Stock & Drag Illustrated* track test that produced a 13.97-second/100.2-mile-per-hour time slip. Yes, the car was cumbersome in the turns. But off the line, it was as quick as they came in 1971.

Then as quick as it came it went. Only 1,250 429 CJ/SCJ Mustangs were built for 1971 before the big-block performance option was unceremoniously dropped midyear. Ford tried to keep the name alive by filling the gap for the remainder of 1971 with the low-compression 351 Cobra Jet small block. But this Cleveland small block, rated at 280, wasn't worthy. Not even close. Most today don't even remember the 351 CJ. But no one will ever forget the 428 and 429 Cobra Jets.

CHAPTER 7

AT THE SPEED OF SOUND

Mach 1 Mustangs, 1969–1973

Nineteen sixty-nine was a busy year in the Mustang corral. New variations on the pony car theme abounded that year, beginning with the quasi-luxurious Mustang Grande with its semi-regal vinyl roof, definitely deluxe interior, and kinder, gentler suspension. Not kind or gentle in the least were two other new additions to the Mustang lineup. The Boss 429 Mustang was a 375-horsepower big-block bomb best suited to short bursts of awesome speed—say, about 1/4 mile in length. Its little brother, the small-block Boss 302, was a nimble, high-winding road rocket able to handle twists and turns with aplomb. Following hot on the heels of the 428 Cobra Jet, the two Bosses overnight vaulted the Mustang toward the head of the musclecar pack, a place where many among the Ford faithful felt Detroit's first pony car should have been kicking up its heels from the beginning.

Not all Mustang drivers, however, wanted to dash away from the field every time they got behind the wheel. Many preferred to simply look the part of a race leader. Can you blame them? Owning and operating a high-performance automobile in the 1960s and early 1970s always represented a compromise. No pain, no gain clearly applied. While the two Boss Mustangs were certainly fun to drive at their limits, they were also bone-jarring, loud, hot-headed beasts in everyday traffic. These cars weren't suited for everyone, just people who were suited for them.

Nor did Ford intend them for everyone. Total Boss 429 production for 1969 and 1970 was only 1,358. After unloading 1,628 Boss 302s in 1969, Ford did roll out another 7,013 in 1970. But while that latter figure may look large, all things are relative—it represented only 3.6 percent of total Mustang production that

Above: The tape stripes, dual color-keyed racing mirrors, quad exhaust outlets, and styled-steel wheels were all standard Mach 1 features in 1969. The competition-style pop-open gas cap was also part of the deal. The rear wing and window slats were options.

Left: The new Mach 1 SportsRoof, introduced in 1969, was everything the GT had been before and more. Heavy-duty handling was standard, as was an image that screamed speed, even while standing still. Adding hot options like the ram-air 428 Cobra Jet, shown here, backed up all those hot looks with serious performance.

The 1969 Mach 1's hood was almost completely blacked out. Racing-style hood pins with cable lanyards were standard, too. The Shaker scoop was optional—a nonfunctional hood scoop was included in the basic Mach 1 package.

Ford introduced this type of styled-steel wheel in 1968. It then became a standard Mach 1 feature with chrome plating instead of argent paint in 1969. The F70-14 tire was a mandatory option whenever the 428 Cobra Jet big block was ordered.

year. A similar situation applied to the GT Mustang. It, too, was a goer. Yet its cut of the annual production pie never rose beyond 5.5 percent, which again was nothing unexpected in Dearborn. Putting one in every garage wasn't part of the plan.

That plan changed when Ford introduced a fourth new Mustang model for 1969, the Mach 1. The sporty Mach 1 effectively replaced the GT atop the Mustang pecking order, and it did so in a big way. While Ford's last GT was quietly rolling into the sunset, the first Mach 1 was reinventing pony car popularity. Production was a whopping 72,458 that first year. That figure fell just 15,000 short of the GT's *total* 1965 to 1969 run.

The Mach 1's sensational start out of the chute wasn't tough to explain. This new breed appealed to a much wider customer base than its GT forerunner and the two Bosses. Unlike its Boss brethren, the Mach 1 wasn't totally intended for those who lived life in the who-cares-about-comfort-and-convenience fast lane. Like the upscale Grande, the Mach 1 was treated to an extra 55 pounds of sound insulation and deadeners to help keep the peace inside. Its interior was also loaded with classy, comfortable features. But there was an alter ego too. The car had no problem raising a little hell on demand thanks to the GT Handling Suspension included as standard equipment.

High-performance imagery came standard in spades, inside and out. For starters, the Mach 1 was based on the restyled, renamed SportsRoof body. Mustang 2+2s had always impressed critics with their sporty flair, but this new variation on the fastback theme really had them buzzing about its sleek, sexy shape and competition-inspired touches. Although neither was functional, the "brake" scoops

behind the doors and that ducktail rear end made the car at least look like it meant business. Additional racing-style treatments then ensured that the Mach 1 would be impossible to miss. In *Car and Driver*'s words, the look was "a blend of dragster and Trans-Am sedan."

Nearly all of the Mach 1's hood and cowl were blacked out, and a trendy—albeit nonfunctional—scoop adorned the former. Integrated turn signal indicator lights were added to that scoop's trailing edge, and competition-type hood pins graced the hood's leading edge. To keep those pins from "walking off," they were attached to the car by plastic-coated cable lanyards. Customers who preferred not to fool with the cool-yet-clumsy pins could have them deleted by request.

Additional competition imagery included dual color-keyed racing mirrors and a pop-open gas cap in back. Jazzy tape stripes with "Mach 1" identification were added to the lower bodysides and across the lip at the back of the decklid. These stripes came in three color combinations depending on the paint chosen: black with gold accent, red with gold accent, and gold with white accent.

Bright rocker moldings were standard too. Even brighter were the styled-steel wheels with their chrome center caps and trim rings. These GT-style rollers (with plain center caps) were the only type offered for the first Mach 1. Standard tires were E70x14 white-sidewall fiberglass-belted Wide Ovals. F70 Wide Ovals, both belted and radial, were optional depending on engine

choice. A Mach 1 could be jazzed up even further with three other popular options: the front chin spoiler, rear window slats, and rear spoiler, all made popular on the Boss 302.

Sporty impressions continued inside where every classy Mustang interior option was included. New high-back bucket seats fitted with "Comfortweave" knitted-vinyl inserts were standard, as was a center console and floor shifter. The steering wheel was the deluxe three-spoke "Rim-Blow" type normally included in the Interior Decor Group option offered for non-Mach 1 Mustangs. The rest of this group's features were also standard in Mach 1s. Along with the seat inserts and the deluxe wheel, these touches included bright pedal trim, a large rally-type clock inset into the instrument panel's passenger side, and a full dose of simulated teak-wood-grain appliques. This faux wood treatment appeared on the dash, console, and door panels. Door panels also featured courtesy lamps.

The base 351 Windsor was an easy-to-live-with 250-horsepower small block topped by an economizing two-barrel carburetor. Available at extra cost were the 290-horsepower 351-4V, the 320-horse 390 big block, and the 335-horse 428 Cobra Jet with or without ram-air equipment. Choosing the ram-air Cobra Jet meant trading the Mach 1's standard, purely ornamental hood scoop for the famed, fully functional Shaker air cleaner assembly. Dual exhausts with chromed quad outlets were included with all four of the Mach 1's optional four-barrel V-8s.

The whole idea was to make the Mach 1—like the Mustang itself—many different cars for many different buyers. The limited-production CJ big-block option was for leadfoots who cared about little else besides stomping out the competition in stoplight derbies. The much more popular 351 Mach 1, meanwhile, was a classy, comfortable cruiser with a sporty flair all but unmatched in its field. Could more than 70,000 customers have been wrong?

Sales cooled down to 40,970 in 1970, but the raves just kept on coming. "Even though the Boss 302 has to rank as the ultimate in Mustangs, the Mach 1 runs a close second," announced a September 1969 *Sports Car Graphic* report. "And for the difference in bucks and cop-attraction, you might want to take another look at the Mach 1." The base price for a Boss 302 in 1970 was

$3,720. The standard Mach 1, powered by the 250-horsepower 351-2V, cost $3,271 that year.

The new four-barrel-fed Cleveland V-8 was next up, priced at $48. Its free-breathing canted-valve heads promised even better performance for the small-block Mach 1 in 1970. Output for the 351 Cleveland 4V was 300 horsepower.

The optional 390 FE big block didn't return, but the big, bad 428 CJ did. Again, dual exhausts with chromed outlets—ovals this time—were included behind the four-barrel V-8s. And the Shaker ram-air option was available for all V-8s, not just the Cobra Jet. Also new for 1970 was a rear stabilizer bar for the standard heavy-duty suspension. The E70 rubber, dual color-keyed racing mirrors and a competition-style pop-open gas cap made encore appearances as standard equipment for the second-edition Mach 1.

Additions to that list included a special plastic grille with unique driving lights and a black honeycomb rear panel applique. Large extruded aluminum moldings with dark accents and diecast "Mach 1" letters also appeared along each rocker panel. The hood pins and lanyards used in 1969 were replaced by simpler twist-type hood

The Mach 1 interior featured high-back bucket seats with "Comfortweave" knitted-vinyl inserts, loads of simulated wood paneling, a deluxe Rim-Blow three-spoke steering wheel, a console, and a rally-type clock on the passenger end of the dashboard.

Mach 1 exterior treatments were revised for 1970. Most noticeable were the finned aluminum rocker panel moldings with diecast "Mach 1" lettering. Engine displacement tape stripes were also added to the hood.

A mag-style wheel cover became standard at the corners for the 1970 Mach 1. This wheel cover was optional for other Mustangs that year, including the Boss 302.

latches, and the styled-steel wheels were traded for simulated mag-type Sport wheel covers.

Revisions were made to the paint and tape accents as well. The blacked-out hood treatment was reduced to a paint stripe barely wider than the nonfunctional scoop. This paint was either low-gloss black or white, depending on the exterior finish. Thin tape stripes incorporating engine displacement lettering bracketed that paint. A wide decklid tape stripe, also done in black or white, was interrupted in the middle to make

The color-keyed bumper and matching fender caps were new Mach 1 features for 1971. The functional ram-air hood, chin spoiler, and Magnum 500 wheels were options. Conventional steel wheels with flat center caps and trim rings were standard.

Introduced in April 1971, the Sports Hardtop borrowed some of the Mach 1's image to offer Mustang buyers a more affordable way to look cool. *Ford Motor Company, photo courtesy of* Automobile Quarterly

room for large diecast "Mach 1" letters. Minor changes were also made to the interior, but the main attractions there carried over from 1969.

Save for the basic image, next to nothing carried over into 1971. Bunkie's big baby may have grown in size, but both the third-edition Mach 1's base engine and corresponding standard equipment list shrank—this while the car's base price went up $200 to $3,474.

First and foremost, the sporty, luxury-laden crew compartment was gone, at least for customers who wouldn't or couldn't shell out the extra dough for the Mach 1 Sports Interior, now a $130 option. Available for all SportsRoof models in 1971, this interior package included such familiar items as bright pedal trim, special carpet with sewn-in rubber floor mats, simulated wood treatment (on door panel inserts and the dashboard's center instrument panel), and those knitted-vinyl high-back buckets, which were thinner and trimmer compared to the seats used in 1970. An electric clock was a part of the deal too, but this time it was found in the left-hand instrument pod in front of the driver. Both that pod and its right-hand counterpart were surrounded by a black applique. The instrument panel mounted above the console was fitted with an ammeter and oil and temperature gauges. Molded door panels, with integrated handles and armrests, completed the deal. A console and the deluxe three-spoke Rim-Blow steering wheel became options in 1971. A deluxe two-spoke tiller was the steering wheel of choice in the Mach 1 interior.

At least a heavy-duty foundation with front and rear sway bars, now called the Competition Suspension, was still included in 1971. So too were twin color-keyed racing mirrors and dual exhausts with round extensions for the Mach 1's four-barrel V-8s. A restyled pop-open gas cap brought up the rear.

E70x14 white-sidewall tires were standard for small-block Mach 1s in 1971. F70 rubber came along with an optional big block. Truly fat F60x15 white-letter rubber was available at extra cost in all cases. These tires required another option, the attractive 15x7 Magnum 500 wheels. These chromed five-spokes were easily the snazziest Mach 1 rims to date and perhaps were even better-looking adornments than the 14-inch styled-steel wheels of 1965 and 1967. You make the call. Standard at the corners for the 1971 Mach 1 were 14x7 rims dressed with flat center caps and deep-dish

Like the grille, the 1971 Mach 1's rear cove panel was a blacked-out honeycomb unit. Bright-tipped dual exhausts were standard, but only when a 351-4V small block or 429 Cobra Jet big block was ordered. A 302-2V was the 1971 Mach 1's base engine.

A typical Mustang hood without scoops was included in the 1971 Mach 1 deal with the standard 302 small block. The twin-scooped "NASA" hood was a no-cost option for the 302 Mach 1, and was automatically included whenever a 351 or 429 CJ was installed. Those twin scoops only became functional when the ram-air option was specified.

trim rings. Sport wheel covers like those used by the 1970 Mach 1 were also optional in 1971.

Additional 1971 Mach 1 appearance items included a black honeycomb grille mounting a pair of rectangular "sportslamps" just inboard of each headlight. A black honeycomb applique was also added at the tail. Taping was limited to a typical horizontal triple-stripe across the tail. A "Mach 1" decal joined that stripe in back, and "Mach 1 Mustang" decals were slapped on the fenders. Bright lower bodyside moldings were added to set off contrasting paint (black or argent, again depending on body color) applied below that trim. This paint also extended around each corner onto the front and rear valance panels.

While a conventional chromed bumper remained in back, the front unit was molded in urethane and colored to match exterior paint. Color-keyed moldings also replaced the bright fender caps and leading-edge hood trim found on non-Machs in 1971. A popular option that helped contrast that monochromatic look up front was a bodyside tape stripe that ran the length of the car, tapering off at the tail.

These stripes were standard for the Boss 351 Mustang in 1971, and they were also used on the little-known

Sports Hardtop, a sales promotional model introduced in the spring of 1971. This coupe was dressed up further with the Mach 1's honeycomb grille, lower bodyside paint, and color-keyed urethane bumper. A nonfunctional NASA hood was included too.

Beneath the hood on a bare-bones Mach 1 in 1971 was a downsized small block—the 302 two-barrel Windsor V-8, rated at 210 horsepower. According to a Ford announcement, the meek little 302 was dropped into the standard package "to broaden the Mach 1's potential market appeal." Apparently a bold, blacked-out bonnet limited that appeal, for a 302-powered Mach 1 came standard with a typical 1971 SportsRoof hood—no scoops, functional or otherwise; no accent, black or argent, wide or thin. No worry, though. The so-called "NASA " hood was a no-cost option atop the standard small block.

This hood was included in the Mach 1 package whenever an optional V-8 was ordered in 1971. It featured twist-type locks and an accent stripe down the center done once more in either black or argent. Added as well to this lid were the two NACA-duct scoops that inspired the "NASA" misnomer used by Ford's hype-happy labelmakers.

The optional 351 Cleveland four-barrel small block was rated at 285 horsepower in 1971. Notice the plastic ram-air ductwork on the hood's underside.

Like the standard scoop in 1969 and 1970, these ducts were not functional in base form. Putting them to work drawing in cooler, denser outside air required adding the Dual Ram Induction option, which replaced the protruding Shaker. Like the Shaker, this equipment worked too, as good air was rammed into the carburetor, freeing up extra ponies on the top end.

The Dual Ram Induction hood was included along with the Mach 1's top optional engine in 1971, the new 385-series Cobra Jet big block, the 429 CJ-R. A "standard" 429 CJ topped by a nonfunctional NASA hood was also available. As was the case with the 428 Cobra Jet, a Super Cobra Jet 429 variety was offered in 1971. But this time the SCJ version was rated 5 ponies higher than its CJ brother—375 horses for the 429 Super Cobra Jet with or without ram-air equipment. Both 428 Cobra Jets, Super or not, were rated at 335 horsepower in 1969 and 1970. A non-ram-air 429 Cobra Jet in 1971 also wasn't advertised any differently whenever it was transformed from CJ to CJ-R—a 370-horse label was used in both cases. One difference, though, came at the ground where the CJ's standard F70 tires were dressed up with white letters for the CJ-R. White-letter rubber was optional for the 429 Cobra Jet without ram-air.

Dual Ram Induction was available at extra cost for the 1971 Mach 1's two optional small blocks, the 2V and 4V 351 Cleveland V-8s. Advertised output for the former was 240 horsepower, 285 for the latter. The hot, little high-winding Cleveland again represented a good choice as far as optimum all-around performance was concerned.

Physical laws didn't change after 1970, and the heavier 1971 Mustang was still radically nose-heavy when the 429 was installed. The car's 60/40 front/rear weight gave it the same limitations when traveling fast in the twisties. "Nobody makes a 7-liter front-engined car that corners well," explained an October 1970 *Sports Car Graphic* road test of the 1971 Cobra Jet Mach 1. "We'll just have to concede that it ain't no sports car—it's more of a straight-liner."

But what a "straight-liner." The 429 SCJ-R Mach 1 qualified as one of the fastest musclecars ever unleashed by Ford engineers. It was also short-lived. Dearborn slammed the door shut on big-block high performance in 1971, leaving the 351 Cleveland to do all the high-profilin' from then on.

As for impressions standing still, the 1971 Mach 1 inspired a mixed bag of responses. Ford's new "flat-back" SportsRoof body got a love/hate reception. There was no middle ground. According to *Motor Trend*'s Bill Sanders, the "Mach 1 is back in force, its sleek, exciting fastback creating the appearance of power in motion." Other critics weren't so sure, and the bulk of their complaints involved the car's heavy impressions, which made it appear like it gained even more weight than it actually had. They also didn't like the poor rearward visibility. Most witnesses, though, couldn't deny that the car could turn heads with ease, and that wasn't a bad thing. As *Sports Car Graphic*'s review concluded, "Whatever it isn't, it is exciting, and even in these troubled times no Mach 1 is going to rust in a showroom." Mach 1 production in 1971 remained healthy at 36,499 units.

A nearly identical Mach 1 Mustang returned for 1972 wearing a lower base sticker of $3,003. "The car has been only refined from the successful 1971 entry," claimed Ford paperwork. The one quick way to identify the 1972 Mach 1 was to look in back, where a pop-open gas cap was no longer used. In its place was a standard Mustang cap.

All other standard equipment carried over from 1971, including the base 302-2V small block, now net-rated at 141 horsepower. Again, the NASA hood wasn't included atop the 302 unless specified as a no-cost option. It was added automatically along with the three optional Cleveland small blocks, the 177-horse 351-2V, the 351-4V Cobra Jet, and the top-dog 351-4V HO. As before, only the four-barrel 351s were fitted with the brightly tipped dual exhausts.

The rare 351 HO (High Output) of 1972 was basically a tamed version of the small-block of the same name used exclusively by the Boss 351 Mustang in

1971. Ford engineers hoped to keep the Boss engine alive in a world fueled on unleaded gasoline even if the Boss Mustang itself was no longer around to benefit from their efforts. But the 351 HO V-8 almost didn't survive past 1971, either. *Car and Driver* explained the situation in its March 1972 issue:

"Obviously there had a been a battle over the 351 HO. The accountants can't justify that kind of car anymore and they've let everybody know it. Performance cars run against the strictly functional grain of many buyers nowadays, and there is a kind of overriding fear that mud-slinging consumer advocates might hold up a new performance car as proof that the engineering department isn't spending every minute of its waking time on anti-smog and safety devices. With such a cloud blocking the sun, the persuasive tongue of the product planning department has had to work overtime to get the 351 HO out of committee and into action. By the time that political task was

accomplished, a mid-year introduction was the best anybody could hope for."

According to engineer Tom Morris of Ford's Special Engine Group, "the basic guts" of the two HO small blocks were the same, with different cylinder heads, pistons, and camshaft incorporated in 1972. The Boss 351's beefy short-block assembly—featuring four-bolt main bearing caps, a cast nodular-iron crankshaft specially selected for superior grain structure, and heavy-duty magnafluxed connecting rods shot-peened for extra hardness—carried over for the still-durable 1972 HO. So did the aluminum dual-plane intake manifold, which sported a big Autolite four-barrel carburetor.

The pistons remained forged-aluminum pieces, but were more of a flat-top design compared to their Boss 351 counterparts. This was done to help lower compression so the new low-octane unleaded fuels wouldn't cause predetonation. The ratio was 8.8:1, down from the 1971 HO's molecule-mashing 11:1, but still a relatively high number considering the compression cuts rampant in Detroit in 1972.

Like its Boss forerunner, the 1972 HO's cam was a mechanical unit, but it was tamed considerably to work with the lowered compression. While the second-edition HO's solid-lifter bumpstick actually had more lift—0.491 inch compared to 0.477 for the Boss 351—it was ground for less duration. Overlap between intake and exhaust turns was lowered from 58 degrees to 35 to improve combustion for the lighter squeeze in the new HO's chambers, which were also revised. The Boss 351's wedge heads were traded for the 351 Cobra Jet's open-chamber pieces—more on these in a moment. All this added up to 275 maximum horsepower at 6,000 rpm.

At the track, those numbers in turn translated into a quarter-mile run of 15.1 seconds at 95.6 miles per hour, according to the March 1972 *C/D* test—a far cry from the mid-13-second blasts recorded by the Boss 351 the year before. But there was an understandable excuse. "In terms of straight-line power the muscles have atrophied in the past 12 months," began *Car and Driver*'s explanation. "Emissions come first these days, power second." After another 12 months, Mustang buyers with a serious need for speed would be begging for that much straight-line power anyway. By then the 351 HO was history, and there wasn't anything on the horizon to take its place.

Yet there was one last performance survivor, another Cleveland small block derived from the Boss 351's power source. According to *Popular Hot Rodding*, the 351 Cobra Jet was "an attempt at 'cross-breeding' the standard Cleveland 4V (285 brake horsepower and 10.7 compression) and the truly high-performance Boss 351 (330 brake horsepower and 11.0 compression). The difference between these two engines is like night and day, but we must applaud Ford on its strategy with the new CJ." Actually introduced very late in the 1971 model run (it was announced in May that year), the 351 Cobra Jet reportedly replaced the existing 351-4V. It didn't officially appear in Ford paperwork until the 1972 lineup was announced. As the *PHR* testers partially explained, the idea was to offer a decent fraction of the Boss 351's HO brand of performance at a lower cost.

Like the 1972 HO, the 351 CJ borrowed the Boss 351's burly cylinder block with its four-bolt main bearing caps. Typical 351 Clevelands, if you will remember, used two-bolt blocks. The crankshaft, on the other hand, was the same cast-iron unit bolted up by those two-bolt caps on 2V and 4V Cleveland V-8s, not the high nodularity cast crank inside the 351 HO. Instead of the forged-aluminum pop-up pistons stuffed into the HO, the 351 CJ was filled with cast-aluminum flat-top slugs. The fuel/air squeeze for the small-block CJ was also 8.8:1.

Cobra Jet cylinder heads were based on the 351-2V's open-chamber design, but used the 351-4V's larger valves: 2.19-inch on the intake, 1.71 on exhaust. The cam was a hydraulic grind with 270 degrees of intake duration, 290 degrees exhaust. Overlap was 46 degrees. Valve lift was also aggressive at 0.48 inch. Ignition was supplied by a dual-point distributor that was basically a recalibrated version of the spark trigger used by the 351 HO. The Cobra Jet's dual-plane intake manifold was also similar to the one used by the Boss 351's HO small block, but it was cast in iron instead of aluminum. This intake was topped by a 4300-D Autolite spread-bore four-barrel.

Output rating for the 351 Cobra Jet was 280 horsepower in 1971. While the cam and compression stayed the same for 1972, a few minor changes (retarded timing to help meet those tightened emissions standards) resulted in a rating drop to 266 horsepower. Apparently the Cobra Jet label was also quietly dropped from official references this year—perhaps to avoid any unwanted attention from both federal antiperformance cops and pesky insurance agents. According to Ford engine lineup lists, the 351 CJ, officially named or not, was fitted with smaller valves in 1973—2.04-inch intakes, 1.65-inch exhausts. Compression, too, went down, to 7.9:1. Advertised output was 259 horsepower.

Curiously, neither the Cobra Jet nor HO 351 could be had with ram-air in 1972. The functional Dual Ram Induction hood was only offered for the two-barrel 351 V-8 that year. Its price dropped too, down from $65.00 in 1971 to $58.24. That the ram-air option was no longer available for the Mach 1's top-performance powerplants again was a matter of meeting Washington's toughened emissions standards. Apparently the 351-4V couldn't meet emissions standards with ram-air, while the tamer two-barrel could. The same situation existed in 1973.

Mach 1 production fell to 27,675 in 1972, but that decrease was mostly the result of a general drop in Mustang sales overall. Total pony car production was down by 16 percent that year. Meanwhile, the Mach 1's percentage of the annual run remained about the same as in years past. The Mach 1's cut was 24.2 percent in 1969, 21.5 in 1970, 24.4 in 1971, and 22.1 in 1972.

The Mach 1's piece of the pie reached an all-time high in 1973 as Mustang sales reversed themselves for one last fling before the first-generation pony car platform was retired. Ford built 134,867 Mustangs for 1973, nearly 10,000 more than were let loose the previous year. Of that total a hefty 26.3 percent, or 35,440 cars, were Mach 1s.

Base price for the 1973 Mach 1 was up slightly to $3,088. Again, the package was all but identical to the previous year's package. The only changes involved new tape stripes that superseded the contrasting lower bodyside paint used in 1972. Located down near where the bright delineation trim was found the previous year, the 1973 side stripes had "Mach 1" identification cut into them just ahead of each rear wheel. "Mach 1" lettering, offset to the passenger side, was also included in the rear deck stripe.

The 302-2V was again standard, and the two 351 Clevelands, the two-barrel and the four-barrel CJ survivor, were optional. A new option for 1973 was a 14x6 forged-aluminum slotted mag that replaced the 15-inch Magnum 500 wheel offered previously. The Sport wheel cover, with its simulated lug nuts, was also still around as a Mach 1 option. But by 1973, the big Sports Roof Mustang wasn't.

Nonetheless, Ford continued marketing the Mach 1 image after the first generation came to a close in 1973. The Mustang II model lineup included a Mach 1 up through that generation's last year in 1978. It wasn't the same, of course. When the compact Mustang II was mercifully scrapped, so too was the Mach 1, undoubtedly never to return. The GT was reborn in 1982, and continues running strong. But unlike in the Mach 1's heyday, one top-shelf, performance-oriented Mustang is enough for the modern market.

CHAPTER 8

LARGE AND IN CHARGE

Boss Mustangs, 1969–1971

Like Lee Iacocca, Bunkie Knudsen was well aware of just how influential the youth market had become in the 1960s. Bunkie, in fact, actually had beaten Iacocca to the punch as far as targeting younger buyers was concerned. Or at least the younger at heart. Himself General Motors' youngest ever general manager at the time, Knudsen was only 43 when he became Pontiac's chief in June 1956. Then, almost overnight, he transformed your grandpa's car company into a builder of true excitement. "You can sell a young man's car to an old man," went his prime motto, "but you'll never sell an old man's car to a young man."

Knudsen loved young men's cars. He loved racing too. Thus, it was little wonder that Pontiacs were soon running with the hottest machines on American roads in 1957. Pontiacs also began winning on stock car tracks in 1958. And the hits just kept on coming. Thanks to Bunkie's speed-sensitive leadership, Pontiacs became kings of the drag strip in 1960, then went on to

thoroughly dominate the NASCAR circuit in 1962. By then, however, Bunkie had taken his bag of tricks elsewhere. In November 1961 he moved over to Chevrolet to continue pumping up a performance image there.

When Knudsen arrived in Dearborn in February 1968, one of his main goals was to put Ford back into the race—on the street. Both Pontiac and Chevrolet had obviously benefited from his quick thinking, why not his new employer? Iacocca could complain all he wanted, but one plain truth still prevailed: Hot cars still turned heads, at least for the moment. As long as Americans had a need for speed, Bunkie was going to give it to them.

The 428 Cobra Jet Mustang was already waiting in the wings when Henry Ford II hired Knudsen. But, in Bunkie's opinion, there was no reason to stop there. In the CJ Mustang, Ford clearly had an able rival to Chevrolet's SS 396 Camaro and Pontiac's Firebird 400 HO. Knudsen, however, knew that there was more to the pony car performance game than just burning up the quarter-mile. Chevy engineers in 1967 had also created

Above: Boss 302 production in 1969 was 1,628. The figure soared to 7,013 after SCCA racing rulemakers raised the minimum production limit for cars slated for Trans-Am competition. *Ford Motor Company, photo courtesy of* Automobile Quarterly

Left: Stodgy Ford execs may not have understood the name at first, but cool kids on the street knew exactly where the Boss Mustang was coming from. Dearborn introduced the Boss 302, along with its Boss 429 big-block brother, in 1969. Shown here is the 1970 Boss 302.

The ultra cool Shaker scoop became a Boss 302 option in 1970. Beneath that black scoop is the high-winding Cleveland-head small block that was conservatively rated at 290 horsepower.

Adding Larry Shinoda's rear wing to the Boss 302's trunk lid also added weight, meaning a prop rod had to be installed to hold the lid in place in the open position. Notice the space-saver spare tire.

another hot Camaro, a nimble little screamer that picked up where Carroll Shelby's original GT 350 left off. Built with SCCA Trans-Am road racing in mind, the legendary Z/28 instantly became the best of its breed as far as all-around performance was concerned. It could handle as well as haul ass.

Knudsen wasn't above stealing things from his former employer—that Ford's restyled 1970 Thunderbird

incorporated a pronounced beak reminiscent of a Pontiac's prow was no coincidence. More than one GM genius also jumped over to Ford at Bunkie's invitation. And, like Bunkie, they brought more than one GM idea along with them. Perhaps the most notable defector, from a Mustang fan's perspective, was designer Larry Shinoda, the man who had drawn up the sensational 1963 Sting Ray for Bill Mitchell and Zora Duntov. Among other feathers in his cap while at Chevrolet were various showcars, including both Mako Sharks (I and II) and the Corvair Monza GT. The Z/28's image was his work as well.

At Ford, Shinoda was assigned the task of not just copying the Trans-Am Camaro, but doing it one better. He was hired by Knudsen in May 1968 and then made head of Ford's Special Projects Design Office, where one of his jobs was to create a special new look for the special new Mustang then being hurriedly developed for 1969. Interestingly, the former GM man admitted he had not been impressed by Ford's pony car. At first. "Initially [we] thought—well, all it is is a Falcon," said Shinoda in a 1981 *Mustang Monthly* interview. "Then it started selling like crazy. We said, well we have our Monza. The Monza did sell better than the basic Corvair, but it was still a sewing machine against the Mustang. The Mustang had the right image, and Chevrolet was forced to build the Camaro." Four years later, Shinoda found himself in the unique situation of upstaging the racy Camaro image he had helped create.

Shinoda's contributions to the new Mustang's image came twofold. The stripes, slats, and spoilers he designed caught the eye, while the name he campaigned for was soon on every street machine lover's lips. "They were going to call it 'SR-2,' which stood for 'Sports Racing' or 'Sports Racing—Group II,' which I thought was a dumb name," remembered Shinoda in 1981. His better choice was borrowed from the cool West Coast lexicon of the day. "I suggested they call it 'Boss,'" he continued. "Chevrolet had already named their Trans-Am Camaro the Z/28, but to try to emulate them by calling the new Mustang the 'SR-2'? Well, it was sure not going to help the image of the new vehicle."

Shinoda's superiors initially had a tough time relating to "Boss"—because they were too old and square perhaps? But once they were tuned in as to how hip it

was to be boss, they jumped back, Jack. And thus the Boss Mustang was born.

Actually two Boss Mustangs came into this world in 1969, and both were developed concurrently by Ford's performance contractor, Kar Kraft Engineering, in Brighton, Michigan. Kar Kraft began building Boss prototypes in August 1968. The first of these went together in only three weeks after Knudsen demanded that his engineers produce "absolutely the best-handling street car available on the American market." This

machine would evolve into the Boss 302, Ford's response to the Z/28 Camaro, both on the street and at SCCA Trans-Am racing venues. The other, the big, bad Boss 429, was an entirely different kind of animal. Created to legalize the "Blue Crescent" 429 V-8 for NASCAR competition, this big-block beast, like the Cobra Jet Mustang, was best suited for straight-line speed runs.

Once established in prototype forms, these two polar opposites were then assigned deservedly separate

Designer Larry Shinoda's graphics and quasi-functional add-ons suited the Boss 302 image to a T. Among the latter were a standard chin spoiler up front and the optional window slats and deck lid spoiler in back. The Magnum 500 wheels were also optional.

development teams. The Kar Kraft crew, lead by Roy Lunn, kept the Boss 429 for their own, while Ford Engineering took over full control of the Boss 302 project. It was Tom Feaheny of Ford's Light Vehicle Powertrain Development Section who was originally on the receiving end of Knudsen's demand for a hot-handling Mustang. Feaheny then passed the buck onto chief Light Car engineer Howard Freers, who assigned the job to the best man available, Matt Donner. Donner, principal ride and handling engineer for both the Mustang and Cougar lines, had been working with pony car suspensions from the beginning and also had contributed a clue or two to the Ford/Mercury SCCA racing teams. He knew the underside of the Mustang as well as anyone. Shinoda shared the vehicle dynamics and skid pad testing experience he'd gained at GM.

The Boss 302 suspension package developed by Donner involved, in his words, "mostly adjustments." He kept the geometry basically the same as a standard Mustang's layout, with the most notable change coming in the size of the car's footprint. Putting more rubber on the road and keeping it fully planted there is the first rule of maximizing chassis performance. To this end, Donner chose super fat F60 Wide-Oval tires mounted on wide 15x7 Magnum 500 wheels. To make room for all that extra tread, the Boss 302's front wheel arches were re-rolled to increase clearance. Donner additionally had to develop beefier front spindles to handle the increased cornering loads resulting from the Wide Ovals' stronger grip. Upper control arm mounting points were initially taxed beyond their limits in prototype applications, so extra bracing was added to the shock towers. This bracing soon became a standard feature as well for any Mustang fitted with F60 rubber and the Competition Suspension option.

The rest of the Boss 302's standard suspension typically featured increased-rate springs: 350 in-lb in front and 150 in-lb in back. Gabriel supplied the stiffened shocks, which were staggered (one mounted in front of the axle, the other behind) at the tail to help control axle windup. A thick 0.85-inch stabilizer bar was originally slated for the Boss 302's nose, but was traded for a 0.72-inch unit after a sway bar planned for the rear didn't make it into production. Race-car–quick 16:1 manual steering was standard, as were big 11.3-inch front disc brakes. Ten-inch drums handled braking

chores in back. Power assist for both the brakes and steering was optional.

Power beneath the hood came from a screaming small block that basically represented plan B as far as SCCA competition was concerned. Plan A was to use the short-lived 302 tunnel-port V-8, which was introduced for Trans-Am racing in 1968. The tunnel-port reportedly put out about 450 horsepower, but it couldn't stay together at high rpm. Nor was it ever built in numbers great enough to qualify it as a regular-production engine, something Trans-Am rules specified. None were ever installed in street-stock Mustangs, and it is doubted that any were ever sold "in a crate" over a dealers' parts counter, either. Rules enforcement also entered into Ford's decision to change plans. Although SCCA officials looked the other way concerning existing homologation standards in 1968, new rules the next year couldn't be ignored. Ford would have to build at least 1,000 1969 Boss 302 Mustangs for sale to the public to qualify the model for Trans-Am competition.

Even if it had proven more reliable, the tunnel-port 302 would not have worked for the new Trans-Am Mustang. The exotic engine's huge ports precluded any street-stock application, and high costs ruled out a large production run. The solution for 1969, like the 428 CJ the previous year, involved a clever mixing of existing hardware. Lead engineer Hank Lenox took the 302 tunnel-port's modified four-bolt Windsor-based block and mated it to new cylinder heads then being readied for the 351 Cleveland V-8, the hot small block that Ford would introduce in 1970. With their big ports and large, canted-angle valves, these heads were excellent breathers. Valve size was 2.23-inch/1.71-inch intake/exhaust. Valve gear included solid lifters, hardened pushrods with guide plates, 1.73:1 rocker arms with screw-in studs, and single-valve springs with dampers. Valve lift was 0.477 inch. Duration was 290 degrees for both intake and exhaust.

The rotating assembly began with a hardened, cross-drilled, forged-steel crank. Heavy-duty 3/8-inch rod bolts held eight forged connecting rods to that crank. Forged-aluminum TRW domed pistons squeezed the fuel/air mixture at a 10.5:1 ratio. Factory specifications claimed this assembly was good to 7,000 rpm, but a rev-limiter was included to keep a lid on things by shutting down the juice from the vacuum

Mustangs didn't come any bigger or badder than the Boss 429, offered in limited numbers in 1969 and 1970. Beneath that huge functional hood scoop is the 375-horse "Shotgun" big block with aluminum "semihemi" heads.

advance dual-point distributor at 6,150 revolutions. Other rev-conscious pieces included an underdrive alternator pulley, a baffled 5-quart oil pan, a windage tray below the crank, a balanced water pump impeller, and a five-blade flex fan. Both the fuel and oil pumps were also high-volume. Topping everything off was a huge 780-cfm Holley four-barrel on an aluminum high-rise intake.

Advertised output for the high-winding Boss 302 V-8 was identical to Chevy's figures for the Z/28's 302 V-8: 290 horsepower and 290 ft-lb of torque. Most witnesses quickly recognized that the horsepower figure was conservative to say the least—once again, the idea was to keep insurance agents and safety crusaders at bay. According to engineer Bill Barr, the Boss 302 dyno tested at 314 horsepower with all equipment in place and working. In bare-bones form with no air cleaner and headers in place of the stock exhausts, the Boss 302 produced more than 390 horsepower.

Changing the front suspension geometry meant that the Boss 429 Mustang's fender lips had to be rerolled to make room for the big 15-inch F60 tires mounted on the 7-inch-wide Magnum 500s.

The 15-inch Magnum 500 wheels were standard in the Boss 429's case. Boss 429 Mustang production in 1969 was 857.

Handling all the Boss 302's horses, however many were present, was either a wide- or close-ratio Top-Loader four-speed. Automatics were not available. A heavy-duty nodular 9-inch rear end with 3.50:1 gears and indestructible 31-spline axles was standard. A Trac-tion-Lok differential was optional, as were 3.91:1 and 4.30:1 gears. Cars fitted with either of the last two ratios also required an auxiliary oil cooler.

Completing the standard Boss 302 package was Larry Shinoda's high-profile styling. Even though his superiors pooh-poohed them, Shinoda's front chin spoiler and rear deck wing were added to the already-sleek SportsRoof body. The front spoiler was standard; the rear was an option. Another popular option was Larry's rear window slats, which were every bit as boss-looking as the rest of the car.

Accentuating those quasi-functional add-on pieces were blacked-out paint treatments for the headlight buckets, hood, and cowl up front, and the deck lid and rear cove panel in back. Shinoda cleaned up profile impressions by deleting the standard Mustang Sports Roof's fake rear quarter scoops and roof pillar medallions. He then finished off his masterpiece by adding

Shoehorning the big Boss 429 V-8 into the Mustang's engine bay was only possible after the stock shock towers were reshaped. Front suspension mounting points were then, of course, moved outward. Those wide aluminum heads needed all the room they could get. Notice the oil cooler in front of the radiator (lower left) on this unrestored original 1969 Boss 429.

Squeezing the Boss 429 V-8 into the Mustang was done at the Kar Kraft works in Brighton, Michigan. *Ford Motor Company, photo courtesy of* Automobile Quarterly

Changes to the Boss 429 image in 1970 included a blacked-out hood scoop. That scoop matched the body in 1969. Boss 429 production in 1970 was 499.

As brutally beastly as the Boss 429 Mustang was, its interior was as luxurious as they came in pony car ranks. High-back Mach 1 buckets with their "Comfortweave" knitted-vinyl inserts were standard, as were deluxe seat belts, the three-spoke Rim-Blow steering wheel, and a console.

The Boss 429's battery was moved from the overcrowded engine compartment to the trunk.

reflective C stripes to the bodysides. Reminiscent of the stripes that graced the sides of Ford's dominating GT-40 race cars, these stick-on touches incorporated "Boss 302" identification at their leading edges.

Ford's first Boss 302 rolled off the Dearborn line on April 17, 1969. With at least 290 horses and all the agility of a real road racer, this new Trans-Am pony car was a big hit right out of the gate. *Car and Driver* called it Ford's best handling street car ever, and racked up some impressive times in the quarter-mile—14.57 seconds at 97.57 miles per hour. The Boss was a contender on the track as well, going head to head with the Camaro Z/28. The Camaro took top SCCA honors in 1969, but the Boss 302 prevailed in 1970.

Abiding by SCCA minimum production specifications, Ford built 1,628 Boss 302 Mustangs for 1969. In 1970 the SCCA bumped the minimum requirement to 2,500 cars *or* to 1/250th of a given manufacturer's total production for the previous year, whichever was greater. In Ford terms, this translated into 6,500 Boss 302s for 1970. The true final tally for the year was 7,013.

Updates for 1970 were minimal. Color choices expanded from the four offered in 1969—Bright Yellow, Acapulco Blue, Calypso Coral, Wimbledon White—to 13, including the trio of "Grabber" colors, Grabber Blue, Grabber Green, and Grabber Orange. Accenting any exterior paint choice in 1970 was the blackout treatment front and rear, although the second-edition Boss 302 hood was treated to much less black. Bodyside stripes, again reflective 3M material, were also

revised and now ran up over the fender tops and down the hood. The big Magnum 500 five-spokes were still around but were options in 1970. A second option was a 15-inch version of the Mach 1's mag-style wheel cover. Conventional 15-inch steel rims with flat center caps and trim rings were standard.

Shinoda's front chin spoiler was standard, and the rear spoiler and window slats remained prominent options. A new contribution to the Boss 302 image, the optional Shaker hood scoop, was fully functional and a real attention-getter. Unlike the standard air cleaner in 1969 and 1970, which incorporated a solenoid pop-off valve to allow underhood atmosphere a less-restrictive passage into the carburetor on demand, the Shaker rammed in cooler outside air whenever the pedal hit the metal.

Mechanically the 1970 Boss 302 was identical underneath save for the addition of 1969's planned rear sway bar, which measured 0.687 inch in diameter. With this bar in place, the front stabilizer was then increased in size to 0.85 inch. Additional engineering revisions included a smaller intake valve (2.19 inches) and a

crank that was no longer cross-drilled for extra lubrication. The former was added to help improve the Boss 302 V-8's low-rpm tractability. That latter replacement was made to save money. All other 1970 Boss 302 engine components were 1969 carryovers.

Some 1970 Boss 302 pieces even carried over into 1971. Appropriate decals apparently were prepared before the decision was made to drop the Boss 302 V-8. Clearly, this decision came very late. According to Ford engineer Dick Ronzi, work on the Boss 302's replacement, the 351 HO Cleveland small block, didn't begin until early in 1970—not at all what you would've expected for a product planned for a 1971 release. Then again, engineers wasted little time rushing the Boss 302 Mustang to market—who said they couldn't do the same for its successor? Ford people may have waved a hasty goodbye to the Boss 302 in 1970, but they had its successor, the Boss 351 Mustang, ready to go by that November.

In the meantime, the big-block Boss also had come and gone in a flash—both literally and figuratively. Like its small-block 302 cousin, the Boss 429 Mustang was rapidly developed in late 1968, then quickly and unceremoniously cancelled early in 1970. The Boss 429's demise actually was even more abrupt than the Boss

302's. While both cars only existed because Bunkie Knudsen wanted to keep racing, the Boss 429's ties to the track were tighter. Even with its hot nature and rough ride, a Boss 302 still almost qualified as a daily driver. The Boss 429, however, was by no means suited for the street. Its sole reason for being was to legalize the semi-hemi "Shotgun" motor for NASCAR racing.

NASCAR's production standard didn't specify the vehicle, just the engine. As long as Ford brought at least 500 Boss 429 V-8s to the dance, it didn't matter how they were dressed. On the street, the 429 satisfied homologation demands beneath a Mustang hood. On NASCAR tracks, it then threw its weight around behind the extended snout of Ford's odd-looking Talladega.

The Boss 429 Mustang first hit the streets in January 1969, nearly three months ahead of the Boss 302. Ford began delivering 1969 Mach 1s to the Kar Kraft works in Brighton in December 1968. There the cars were stripped of their engines and stock shock towers. New specially reinforced shock towers were engineered, increasing engine compartment width by 2 inches to make room for the enormous Boss 429 V-8. Upper A-arm location points in turn were moved outward an inch and lowered another inch. Beefier spindles were also installed, as was a modified export brace on top to firmly tie the restructured shock towers to the cowl.

Like the Boss 302, the Boss 429 was fitted with "flared" front fenders. Standard rubber was again the big F60 Wide-Ovals on 15x7 Magnum 500s, with extra clearance supplied by rolling under the lip of the wheel opening. Additional suspension upgrades included super-duty Gabriel shocks (staggered in back, of course) and thick sway bars (0.94 inch front, 0.62 inch rear). Both power front discs and power steering were standard. Also included in the package was a close-ratio four-speed (with a Ford shifter) that delivered torque to a Traction-Lok differential with 3.91:1 gears.

Clearance remained an issue beneath the hood, even with the modified shock towers. A thinned-down power brake booster was used to avoid a conflict on the driver side with the Shotgun motor's huge valve cover. And the battery was relocated to the trunk, where it also conveniently transferred weight from the front wheels to the rears.

Exterior modifications were minor compared to the Boss 302. Unlike the small-block Boss's super-clean shell,

The Boss 429 V-8's 375-horse rating was conservative, but so too was the engine's performance on the street, relative to actual potential. The 735-cfm carb hiding beneath that big air cleaner was itself big, yet it still couldn't feed fuel/air fast enough to those semihemi combustion chambers. The ports were simply too big for the street.

choices. Nearly all other cosmetic touches carried over, with the one notable exception involving the big ram-air hood scoop, which was painted low-gloss black. Mechanical upgrades included the addition of a Hurst shifter and the relocation of the rear sway bar from below the axle to above.

The first 1970 Mustang arrived in Brighton for conversion late in August 1969. The last was not far off. Henry II fired Bunkie less than three weeks later, and Boss 429 production was next on the hit list. Kar Kraft shipped off its final Shotgun-motored Mustang on January 6, 1970. Total Boss 429 production for 1970 was 499. Kar Kraft quietly went away not long after Ford pulled the plug on its racing support in November 1970. Ironically the Brighton works became home to Rectrans, Inc., Bunkie Knudsen's post-Ford venture. Rectrans offered mobile homes designed by Bunkie's buddy, Larry Shinoda.

But not all news in November 1970 was bad. While it would never get the chance to race like its two forerunners, the Boss 351 Mustang was introduced that month to keep the legacy running strong for one more year.

The heart of the 1971 Boss 351 was the 351 HO Cleveland small block, certainly an able standard bearer for the Boss bloodline. Key to the HO were its free-flowing heads, which were nearly identical to those used by the Boss 302 save for revised cooling passages. Sizes for the HO's canted valves were the same as the 1970 Boss 302's. Most of the valvetrain was also identical with screw-in rocker studs, hardened pushrods, and guide plates again making appearances. The Boss 351's solid-lifter cam, however, was more aggressive than the Boss 302's. Duration was truly long at 324 degrees and lift was up to 0.491 inch.

Like the Boss 302's modified Windsor block, the 351 HO's lower end was held together by four-bolt

The final Boss Mustang, the Boss 351, appeared in November 1970, just as Ford was ending its motorsports involvement. Production for the one-hit wonder Boss 351 was 1,806.
Steve Statham

Heart of the Boss 351 Mustang was the 351 HO, a high-compression, solid-lifter Cleveland small block that produced 330 real horsepower. Ram-air equipment was standard.

mains, but the latter had four-bolt caps at all five main bearings, not just three. The HO crank was cast (of high nodular iron) instead of forged, and it was specially tested for hardness. Forged connecting rods were shot peened and magnafluxed and were held to the crank by super-strong (180,000 psi) 3/8-inch bolts. At the working ends of those rods were eight forged-aluminum pop-up pistons. Compression was 11:1. Topping everything off was a 750-cfm Autolite four-barrel on an aluminum dual-plane manifold. The dreaded Autolite rev-limiter was included to help keep a lid on things.

The supporting cast included a ram-induction hood, a special cooling package with a flex fan, and a wide-ratio four-speed controlled by a Hurst shifter. A Traction-Lok 9-inch rear end with 31-spline axles and 3.91:1 gears was standard out back. The Competition Suspension package (heavier springs, staggered rear shocks, front and rear sway bars), F60 raised-white-letter rubber, and power

front discs were included too, as expected. Conventional 15x7 steel wheels adorned with the familiar flat hubcaps and trim rings were standard at the corners. More suitable Magnum 500s were optional.

The list of Boss 351 appearance features was familiar as well, at least to Mach 1 fans. Along with the functional "NASA" hood up front was a chin spoiler and a Mach 1 honeycomb grille with color-keyed surround. The hood featured twist locks and either argent or blackout treatments, depending on body color. Dual racing mirrors, tape stripes, "Boss 351 Mustang" decals, and lower body paint accents adorned the car's sides. Like the hood, those paint accents and the tape stripes were either black or argent, depending on the exterior finish. A black or argent rear panel and another "Boss 351" decal brought up the rear.

Full instrumentation was standard inside. Optional goodies included the Mach 1 sport interior and a rear deck spoiler.

The 351 HO's Cleveland heads featured big ports and flow-conscious canted valves—notice how the valve stems protrude upward at varying angles. Intake valves "leaned" toward their ports, while exhausts did the same in the opposite direction. Less restriction was the end result.

Overall the Boss 351 Mustang was a real winner with the critics. Although most reviewers complained about visibility problems inherent to Knudsen's 1971 SportsRoof restyle, they couldn't deny the Boss 351's aggressive appearance and volatile nature. Few competitors could keep pace. As *Car and Driver* reported, the Boss 351 "offers dragstrip performance [14.1 seconds at 100.6 miles per hour] that most cars with 100 cubic inches more displacement will envy." Enthusiastic *Motor Trend* testers pushed the envelope even further, producing a 13.8-second run, a figure that put the Boss 351 right up there with the hottest Fords ever built.

Most recognized too that the Boss 351 represented Dearborn's swan song in the performance field. "This is probably the last chance you'll have to buy a machine of this kind," began *Sports Car Graphic*'s March 1971 Boss 351 road test. "Ford is now diverting all its racing talent and dollars into solving safety and pollution problems and trying to satisfy government mandates. We have heard from reliable sources that for the '72 new model release, all Ford products will be detuned to run on regular fuel. That means lower compression. The current exhaust-popping 11:1 [ratios] will probably be lowered 15 to 20 percent, and the only way to regain the lost power is through expensive modifications—which will probably become illegal. Perhaps we'll just learn to live with the situation, like war and taxes, which we accept as facts of life. But we have few years left. We might as well take what we can get and live it up while we can."

A few years? The Boss 351 was a one-hit wonder, although the 351 HO small block did survive one more year, detuned. After 1971 the Mustang was again a car that looked like it went fast, yet didn't. Two years later, Lee Iacocca would again have his way. Whether that was good or bad is your call.

EPILOGUE

Celebrating the Rest of the Pony Car Story

Unlike General Motors, Ford seemingly lost interest in birthday parties in the late 1980s and 1990s. It wasn't all that long ago that Dearborn officials were falling all over themselves to honor two decades of pony car history—witness the special-edition 20th anniversary 1984-1/2 Mustangs. Since then, GM has taken advantage of every opportunity to mark its historic moments in grand fashion. Special anniversary models commemorated significant Corvette birthdays in 1988 (35th) and 1993 (40th), and who knows what hoopla awaits the world once the fiberglass two-seater hits a half-century in 2003. Chevrolet also rolled out high-profile orange-and-white 30th anniversary Camaros in 1997. Corporate cousin Pontiac turned a similar trick two years later with its own specially painted

30th anniversary model, this one honoring the only musclecar to run uninterrupted from the 1960s to today—the Firebird Trans Am.

Meanwhile, the original pony car kept rolling on into history with nary a balloon burst or a handful of confetti tossed. Rumors of a super-duper 25th-anniversary Mustang in 1989 led to nothing more than a quasi-commemorative green paint job for a couple thousand custom convertibles quietly built early in 1990. A truly momentous occasion arrived five years later when Ford unveiled the all-new 1994 Mustang, but again no moves were made to celebrate another major milestone. Finally, Ford did mark the Mustang's 35th birthday in 1999 with a commemorative badge for all models and a special exterior/interior dress-up package for a limited number of coupes and convertibles.

Above: Lee Iacocca never did like what happened to the Mustang after 1967. So he tried to re-create history in 1974 with the truly compact Mustang II. *Ford Motor Company, photo courtesy of* Automobile Quarterly

Left: Ford officials basically ignored the Mustang's 30th birthday in 1994, but they chose to mark its 35th anniversary in 1999 with a special options group. Special badging, 17x8 five-spoke aluminum wheels, and a choice of four colors (black clearcoat, silver clearcoat metallic, Crystal White clearcoat, and Performance Red clearcoat) were among the features included in the deal.

What better way to ride up in front of Studio 54 than in a King Cobra. This striped, spatted, and spoiled Mustang II showed up in 1978, just in time to bid farewell to the too-small second-generation pony car. *Ford Motor Company*

That Dearborn officials chose to pass up a couple of wonderful chances to hype the Mustang's longevity can be explained easily enough: They didn't have to. The Mustang is not only the longest-running pony car, it also remains the most popular, having outsold its longtime rival, the Camaro, each year since 1993. By 1997, Ford was beating Chevrolet by nearly a 2 to 1 margin in the pony car sales race, an endurance run that may be nearing the tape. Even as we speak, GM's F-body platform (Camaro/Firebird) is teetering on the brink of extinction due to sagging sales. Ford's Mustang, on the other hand, continues rolling on as strong as ever with 1998 production reaching 161,000, a peak that was surpassed only one other time since 211,225 Mustangs hit the streets in 1988.

Whether or not Dearborn's pony car will follow its F-body rivals into the pits is up to car buyers. Will the dreaded sport-utility vehicle push all other forms of transportation over the edge on the way to hauling the soccer team—or more commonly, a single driver—around town? Only time will tell. In the meantime it looks like Mustang might soon have the market all to itself, just as it did from 1964 to 1966—sorry Plymouth people, but the first-generation Barracuda simply didn't count. As for the key to Mustang's success, it remains so simple. Ford still can't lose with a youthful appeal that attracts such a broad range of customers.

"The Mustang was introduced 35 years ago next April, and the car always has projected an attitude that is free-spirited, fun, and definitely cool," said Ford Division president Jim O'Connor in October 1998. "It's that image and heritage, together with Mustang's straightforward lineup of models and options, that attract a diverse group of buyers. They include women and men about equally, from young people starting out to leading-edge baby-boomers rewarding themselves with some fun and self-expression."

Thirty-five years and counting, who would've thought it?

Regardless of what many purists still believe, Ford didn't stop making Mustangs in 1973. Okay, so the Mustang II did seemingly taint the legacy. Not at first, mind you. It was the bloated models of 1971 to 1973 that were the objects of derision back then. The first Mustang II was an award-winning overnight sales success, at least in 1974. Then, once the novelty wore off, the little compact's welcome wore out. Sure, some collector interest has surfaced in recent years. But the Mustang II continues to be the butt of various jokes among nostalgic followers of the long-hood/short-deck breed. On the other side of the coin, the models that the Mustang II replaced have long since been forgiven for what many Mustangers in the early-1970s perceived as a pure perversion of Lee Iacocca's original ideal. Today, classic Mustang parameters open in 1964 and shut in 1973.

But the story did go on after 1973, and it was Iacocca himself who again gets all the credit (or discredit, depending on your perspective) for what came next. We all know how he felt about his baby growing bigger and heavier in 1967. And his complaints only became louder after Bunkie Knudsen was done with the once-polite pony.

By 1971, Iacocca wasn't the only one doing the bitching. Loyal Mustang buyers were letting their feelings known through the mail. More and more letters were reaching Dearborn in protest of what the Mustang had become. No longer a small, sporty car, it was more of a "luxury bus" as one writer put it.

As early as November 1969, Iacocca had been suggesting a new direction for the Mustang, one that would bring the car back closer to his original plan. Success of the new, compact Maverick in 1970 didn't hurt Iacocca's cause in the least, and it soon became clear his prototype projects would lead to a totally redesigned, downsized Mustang.

Italy's famed design studio, Ghia, was responsible for creating the first working prototype. Ford had bought controlling interest in the Turin firm in November 1970, and within a few months Ghia head Alejandro de Tomaso had turned out a sleek little machine that would lay the groundwork for the development of the first Mustang II. Iacocca's "little jewel" was then officially introduced on August 28, 1973.

Measuring but 96.2 inches from hub to hub, down 13 inches from the 1973 Mustang, the Mustang II was also 4 inches skinnier, 14 inches shorter in overall length, and some 300 pounds lighter. New design features included rack-and-pinion steering, exceptional noise and vibration reduction, and a frugal 2.3-liter four-cylinder engine. A 105-horsepower, 2.8-liter V-6 was optional for the three models offered: a base Mustang II, an upscale Ghia, and the familiar Mach 1. Standard Mach 1 equipment included front disc brakes, a four-speed, bucket seats, and full instrumentation.

Proving that less sometimes is more, the truly small Mustang II set a sales pace nearly as quick as its ancestor had 10 years before. The Arab oil embargo undoubtedly had something to do with the mad rush that developed in the fall of 1973 as many Americans became convinced that small, economical cars were the only way to fly into the future. More than 385,000 buyers chose to take flight behind the wheels of Mustang IIs in 1974, a good number of those perhaps

The new Fox-chassis Mustang was chosen to pace the Indianapolis 500 in 1979. A special run of Indy Pace Car replicas was then produced for public consumption. Both 5.0-liter V-8s (front) and turbocharged four-cylinder (back) versions were built.

Special 1984-1/2 20th anniversary Mustangs were built in both hatchback and convertible forms. *Ford Motor Company*

jumping on the bandwagon after *Motor Trend* named Ford's downsized pony car its "Car of the Year" in January 1974. In *Motor Trend*'s words, the all-new second-generation pony car was "a total departure from the fat old horse of the recent past . . . a rebirth of the Mustang of 1964-65—smaller and even more lithe in feel than the original pacesetter."

Others were not so quick to praise the reborn Mustang. "While the Mach 1's general concept is enthusiast-oriented," claimed *Car and Driver*, "its poor acceleration, wide-ratio transmission and over-weight chassis leave too much of its undeniably sporting

flavor unsupported by nourishment." *Car Craft* called the car "regrettably underpowered," then predicted that Ford would probably have to offer a V-8 version, and soon.

An optional 302 V-8 did arrive in 1975, inspiring a good word or two from *Road & Track*'s John Dinkle. "Rarely can an automobile company take a car designed for a four- or six-cylinder engine, stuff in a heavier, thirstier V-8 and have us liking, much less praising the results," he wrote. "But that's exactly what happened with the 302-equipped 1975 Mustang II." Nonetheless, Mustang II sales for 1975 fell by more than 50 percent.

The SVO Mustang debuted in 1984 to redefine pony car performance. Beneath that off-centered hood scoop was a turbocharged 2.3-liter four-cylinder that pumped out 175 horsepower. *Ford Motor Company*

Not even the revival of the Cobra name could check that trend, as Mustang II sales again dipped in 1976. Soiling a legendary image in many enthusiasts' opinion, the 1976 Cobra II featured front and rear spoilers, rear side window louvers, a simulated hood scoop, aluminum wheels, and lower-body "Cobra II" stripes. Borrowed hype, however, wasn't enough to keep the customer happy. Many had already grown dissatisfied with the car's cramped quarters. It seemed soaring gas prices could only compromise a Mustang buyer's standards so far, a fact demonstrated in 1977 when sales dropped down to the 150,000 plateau, a place not all that much higher than disappointing levels achieved from 1971 to 1973. Sagging sales success then signaled the need for yet another redesigned Mustang.

While work progressed on this project, Ford made one last stab at pumping up the Mustang II image in 1978. Built for five months, the 1978 King Cobra was yet another striped, spoilered, and spatted excuse for a performance car. "With the real muscle-car era now no more than memory," wrote *Car Craft*'s John Asher, "cars like the Ford King Cobra are becoming the machismo machines of the late seventies." Asher's test resulted in a ho-hum 17.06-second/80.69-mile-per-hour quarter-mile pass, embarrassing in early-1970s terms, understandable by late-1970s standards.

Like the Falcon-based original Mustang, the redesigned 1979 model relied on the almost equally mundane Fairmont for its skeleton. This platform was known as the Fox chassis in Ford parlance. Roots of the Fox project—focusing on small, fuel-efficient cars—ran back to 1973 when Middle East affairs were drawing Detroit's attention. Even as the Pinto-based Mustang II was selling like hotcakes, Ford was considering what to do next with its pony car legacy. In

A quarter-century of Mustang history went by almost unnoticed in 1989—no special anniversary model was offered. The special body cladding shown on this 1989 GT convertible first appeared in 1987. It would continue reappearing unchanged up through 1993. *Ford Motor Company*

December 1974, Iacocca gave the go-ahead for the Fox-chassis Mustang.

Per Fox specifications, the next Mustang would of course continue as a rear-driver, although front suspension would come courtesy of a MacPherson strut arrangement. Once Jack Telnack's styling team had completed a crisp, new shell, all that remained was to get the 1979 Mustang to market.

Even though it was wider, longer, and taller than its forerunners, the first Fox-chassis Mustang was 200 pounds lighter than the Mustang II. As for power, the standard 2.3-liter four was joined by a turbocharged four, the 2.8-liter V-6, and the 302 V-8, now recognized as the 5.0-liter. Popular options included the Cobra graphics package and the TRX suspension, the latter featuring attractive aluminum wheels, Michelin metric rubber, and specially tuned springs and shocks.

The sum of the parts added up to an all-new Mustang that represented a refreshing revival of the pony car image. According to *Motor Trend*'s John Ethridge, the 1979 Mustang could "now compete both in the marketplace and on the road with lots of cars that used to outclass it." Initially the car's top power source was the 140-horse two-barrel V-8. But by 1982, a revised 5.0L Mustang would be every bit as quick off the line as GM's Camaro and Corvette. If not quicker.

In honor of the Mustang's impressive revival, the 1979 model was again chosen to pace the Indianapolis 500. Street-going replicas were also offered, both with 5.0L and turbo four power. Special graphics and the TRX suspension were included in the deal.

After temporarily dropping the 5.0L V-8, Ford's 302 small block returned in 1982 as the HO 5.0-liter. Still fed by a two-barrel with a restrictive single exhaust, the 1982 HO nonetheless did pump out 157 net horsepower, more than enough power to suitably complement the GT, which returned after a 13-year hiatus. According to a *Motor Trend* test, the 1982 5.0L GT

Mustangs have paced the Indianapolis 500 every 15 years, and each time the car was a totally new model. In 1994 the Mustang chosen to lead the pace lap at Indy was the Special Vehicle Team's Cobra convertible. All SVT Cobra droptops built that year were Indy Pace Car replicas—adding the door decals was up to the owner. Also shown here is a 1994 SVT Cobra coupe.

could go 0–60 in 6.9 seconds. Such speed qualified as "hot to trot" by early-1980s standards.

Big news in 1983 included the return of a convertible Mustang, which had been in hiding for 10 years, and the addition of a Holley four-barrel for the 5.0L V-8. That Holley helped boost maximum power to 175 horses. Also new was a Borg-Warner T-5 five-speed instead of a four-speed. As they would be in 1984, 1983 GTs were offered with both 5.0L V-8 and nonintercooled turbo four power.

But if a turbocharger was what you wanted, the exciting SVO (Special Vehicle Operations) Mustang was the only choice. Turbocharged and intercooled, the 1984 SVO Mustang's little 140-ci (2.3-liter) four-cylinder pumped out an amazing 175 horses. A Hurst-shifted five-speed, Koni gas-charged shocks, quick steering, four-wheel discs, and 16-inch wheels were also included. Built through 1986, the SVO Mustang received, among other things, a lumpier cam and revised turbo midyear in 1985. These revisions helped bump output up to 205 horsepower. The SVO then was reined back to 200 horses in 1986. Rest to 60 miles per hour in less than seven seconds was no problem for an SVO Mustang. Total production for all models, domestic and imports, was 9,844.

As for the standard Mustang's progression, quad rear shocks appeared in 1984, as did the limited-edition 1984-1/2 20th anniversary model, offered in hatchback or convertible form. Featuring either 5.0L and 2.3L turbo power, the 20th anniversary Mustangs were easily identified by their Oxford White paint with red "G.T. 350" lower body stripes. Ford sold 3,900 20th anniversary hatchbacks and 5,260 convertibles.

In 1985 tubular headers with dual exhausts (from the catalytic converter back) and the 5.0L's first roller cam contributed to a power jump up to 210 horsepower—the highest recorded for a carbureted HO. The following year, the 5.0's four-barrel was replaced by the EEC-IV (electronic engine control) EFI (electronic fuel-injection) system and a true, full-length dual exhaust system. Also new for 1986 was the beefier 8.8-inch rear end, replacing the wimpy 7.5-inch unit used on earlier 5.0L models.

By 1987 much of the Mustang's modern engineering groundwork was complete, leaving only a somewhat tired body to be attended to. Discounting tweaks to the hood and grille and the addition of a spoiler or two, an essentially identical shell had carried over from 1979 to 1986.

Still the same old Fox-chassis Mustang underneath, and retaining the same basic shape and sheet metal, the 1987 Mustang nonetheless took on a definitely new image. Noticeable in the rounded, aero-nose of the base LX models for 1987, the revamped look was far more startling in 1987 GT terms. Along with the LX's "wraparound" headlight arrangement, the 1987 Mustang GT received a complete ground effects skirt treatment and an exclusive lattice taillight design. Unlike the LX, the new GT didn't have a grille opening between the headlights. The GT's new 16-spoke wheels were also exclusives.

Under the 1987 GT's hood was a potent 225-horsepower 5.0L HO V-8 with an enlarged EFI throttle body and improved cylinder heads. A roller cam and tube headers carried over from 1986. LX customers could forgo the standard four-cylinder and opt for the same 5.0L HO, and many did. In the lighter LX body, the 225-horse 5.0L ran an impressive 14.17-scond quarter-mile according to *Hot Rod*. In the same test, a 225-horse 1987 GT tripped the lights in 14.60 seconds. Either way, GT or LX, the 1987 5.0L Mustang was a certified Camaro-killer. And it cost less too.

Recognizing how far their $10,000 would go when spent on a 5.0L LX Mustang, buyers flocked into Ford showrooms in 1988, pushing production of the HO-powered LX from 16,609 the previous year to 30,877. Popularity of the hot 5.0 Mustangs was strong enough to help derail Ford's plan to replace the rear-drive Fox-chassis with a front-drive Mazda platform that instead became the new Probe in 1989. In 1991 new standard 16-inch wheels, requiring revised fenders, replaced the smaller, impossible-to-clean GT rims of 1987 to 1990 and marked the last significant change for the Fox-chassis cars. The last Fox/Mustang rolled out in 1993.

Next came a rebirth of sorts in 1994 that both promised a continuing bright future and reminded many of a historic past. "The wonderful changes that have been made in this automobile will, we feel, bring back this country's love affair with the Mustang," said program manager Mike Zevalkink. "There's a latent passion that wells up in people when they see this car. It's a car for today, but it touches their past in a personal way."

"We brought back a lot of the Mustang heritage in a very contemporary way," added design manager Bud Magaldi. "That seemed to be what people wanted us to do. They didn't want another 1964-1/2 or 1965 Mustang, which they loved. They wanted a new car."

And new it was. Reportedly 1,330 of the car's 1,850 parts were making their debut in 1994. "This is not a carryover platform," said Will Boddie, Ford's Small and Midsize Car Segment director. After spending $700 million on both the car and its assembly plant, Ford started building the 1994 Mustang in October 1993. Official sales startup was December 9.

Underneath was the new Fox-4 chassis, a rigid foundation that improved steering, ride, and handling and also did away with much of the twists and shakes common to the previous platform. A slightly longer wheelbase and wider tread also contributed to the car's newfound surefootedness. And standard four-wheel discs enhanced the attraction even further, as did a 145-horsepower V-6 in place of the old four-cylinder in

The list of improvements made inside and out of the 1994 Mustang is too long to list. Suffice it to say the car was the best-handling, most comfortable Mustang yet.

Thirty years after its birth, the Mustang was treated to a total redesign that left little doubt which car was still out in front of the pony car field. *Ford Motor Company*

Although it was downrated to 215 horsepower, the venerable 5.0 small block was still highly respected on the street in 1994. This long-running pushrod motor was finally replaced by the overhead-cam 4.6-liter V-8 in 1996. *Ford Motor Company*

base models. The tried-and-true 5.0 small block, now rated at 215 horsepower, remained for the GT.

"For at least six years now, Mustang was a terrific engine in search of a better car," wrote *AutoWeek*'s John Clor about Dearborn's latest, greatest pony. "Now it's a better car in search of even more power." "Where the old car got by on its kick-butt, straight-line performance, the new car provides a much more entertaining, better rounded package," chimed in *Road & Track*'s Jim Miller.

Another terrific engine arrived in 1996 as the venerable 5.0L pushrod small-block was traded for the thoroughly modern single-over-head-cam (SOHC) 4.6-liter V-8. It was also rated at 215 horsepower, but had several advantages over its predecessor. It was both lighter and more durable than the 5.0, and it ran noticeably

smoother too. In 1998, Ford boosted the 4.6's horsepower to 225.

Bigger valves, reground cams with higher lift and longer duration, and straighter intake runners contributed to a 35-horsepower increase for the '99 Mustang's 4.6L SOHC V-8. That, however, was just the beginning. Chassis upgrades further improved ride, handling, and steering, and revised floor pan sealing reduced road noise. Convertible platforms were also reinforced to overcome inherent body shakes. On top of it all went a freshened shell, the product of Ford's "New Edge" design school. Chiseled lines and sharp creases replaced the soft contours and compound curves that, according to some critics, allowed the previous body to look very much "Japanese," an impression Ford people had claimed they had tried to avoid at all costs.

Ford's latest pony car looks like nothing else out there. It's not a jellybean, it's certainly not a cube, yet it certainly still is a Mustang. "Our visual theme is based on the most stable geometric form—the pyramid," said chief designer Doug Gaffka. "We've also enhanced or revived some classic Mustang styling cues."

"We've made improvements that are much more than skin-deep," continued chief program engineer Janine Bay. "It all adds up to the fact that the 1999 Mustang really has a lot to offer. Its design is strong, contemporary, and true to Mustang's original concept. Performance improvements make the 1999 models very exciting and satisfying to drive. Make no mistake about it, everything we've done—and will continue to do—makes Mustang better and better, building on its heritage of free-spirited fun in a rear-wheel-drive, all-American sports car."

Special Vehicle Team engineers picked up where Carroll Shelby left off with his GT 350R in 1965, producing a series of race-ready Cobra R models. The first came in 1993 (back), followed by the second in 1995 (right). Only 300 2000 Cobra R models (left) were built, all with 385-horsepower 5.4-liter DOHC V-8s. *Ford Special Vehicle Team*

INDEX

1964 Indianapolis 500, 42
A. O. Smith Company, 104, 106
AMC AMX, 65
AMC Javelin, 65
American Machine and Foundry Company (AMF), 32, 33
American Motors (AMC), 65
American Rodding, 116
AMF Mustang pedal cars, 32, 33
Antonick, Milt, 10
Ash, Dave, 22
Asher, John, 161
Barr, Bill, 114, 115, 118, 123, 125, 145
Bay, Janine, 167
Blue Diamond Classics, 33
Boddie, Will, 165
Bonneville Salt Flats, 14
Bordinat, Gene, 15, 19–21, 24
Brokaw, Jim, 14
Business Week, 32
Car and Driver, 8, 10, 21, 72–74, 78–80, 83, 102, 107, 121, 128, 135, 136, 148, 155, 160
Car Craft, 119, 160, 161
Car Life, 10, 34, 39, 89, 106, 110
Chevrolet Camaro, 11, 54, 64, 69
Chevrolet Corvair Monza, 13, 18, 19
Chevrolet Corvair, 17
Chevrolet Z/28, 64
Cole, Ed, 55, 64
Competition Handling Package, 78
Competition Suspension package, 154
Cummins, Dave, 10
Dahlquist, Eric, 60, 79, 80, 83, 113, 118, 119
De Tomaso, Alejandro, 159
Dearborn Steel Tubing, 56
Decor Interior, 50, 51
Delisio, Randy, 56, 58
DeLorean, John, 64
Dinkle, John, 160
Dodge A/FX, 57
Dodge Challenger, 64
Domestic Special Order (DSO) codes, 51
Donner, Matt, 143
Drag Pack option, 125
Duntov, Zora, 140
Eggert, Bob, 18
Engine
    140-ci 4-cylinder, 164
    170-ci six 6-cylinder, 41, 38
    200-ci 6-cylinder, 38
    260-ci Windsor V-8, 85
    260-ci V-8, 28
    273-ci V-8, 69
    289-ci V-8, 28, 29, 41, 43, 74, 77, 78, 82
    302-ci V-8, 82, 132, 137, 160
    302-ci Windsor, 41, 61, 106, 133
    351-ci (Cobra Jet?), 125, 132, 134, 136
    351-ci, 80, 83, 129, 134
    351-ci Cleveland, 62, 63, 66, 129, 134, 136, 137, 143
    351-ci HO Cleveland, 134, 135, 152, 154, 155
    351-ci Mach 1, 129

351-ci Windsor, 61, 100, 106, 129
390-ci FE V-8, 54, 79, 83, 96, 110
390 Thunderbird Special V-8, 77
390-ci V-8, 102
390-ci,78, 82, 83, 129
427-ci LeMans, 79
427-ci S/C Cobra, 85
427-ci, 96, 97, 114
428-ci Cobra Jet FE-series V-8, 109
428-ci Cobra Jet V-8, 106
428-ci Cobra Jet, 60, 61, 63, 83, 99, 102, 105, 109, 110, 114, 115, 118, 121, 127, 129
428-ci Super Cobra Jet, 115, 121
428-ci, 94, 96, 113
429-ci 385-series, 63
429-ci Blue Crescent, 141
429-ci CJ-R, 134
429-ci Cobra Jet, 119, 121, 123–125, 132
429-ci Super Cobra Jet, 125, 134
5.0 small block, 166
4.6-liter V-8, 166
5.0-literL V-8, 164, 166
5.4-liter DOHV V-8, 167
Blue Crescent, 150
Boss 302 V-8, 61, 63, 145
Boss 302, 61, 63Boss 351, 63
Boss 429 V-8, 61, 63, 146, 149–151Boss 429, 61, 63
Hi-Po 289, 34, 35, 41, 43–45, 47, 69, 70, 72, 74, 75, 78, 88, 91, 92, 94
HO, 162
Taunus 12/15M, 20, 21
Esquire, 27
Estes, Pete, 64
Ethridge, John, 75, 162
Exterior Decor Group, 77
Feaheny, Tom, 59, 143
Follmer, George, 150
Ford Falcon, 14, 17
Ford Galaxie, 56
Ford Mustang Grande, 60, 61
Ford Maverick, 60
Ford Pinto, 60
Ford Stiletto, 21
Ford Thunderbird, 17
Ford Thunderbolt, 56, 57
Ford, Benson, 42, 43
Ford, Henry II, 22, 30, 34, 55, 57, 62, 109, 139, 152
Ford, Henry, 27
Foyt, A. J., 43
France, Bill, 56, 150
Freers, Howard, 143
Frey, Donald, 14, 15, 18, 21, 39, 45, 64, 116
Gaffka, Dough, 167
Geiger, Dave, 56–58
Ghia, 159
Gill, Barrie, 21
Glotzback, 150
Goodell, Fred, 97
Gregson, Dean, 112, 113
GT Equipment Group, 47, 50, 69, 70, 72, 75, 80
GT Handling Suspension, 128
Gurney, Dan, 19, 21

Halderman, Gail, 15, 24, 40, 41, 63
Hamilton, Bob, 58
Harvey, Jerry, 110
Harvey, Scott, 10
Hernandez, Fran, 151
Hertz Rent-A-Car Company, 93, 99
Hertz Sports Car Club, 93
Holman, John, 57
Holman-Moody, 57, 58, 112
Hot Rod, 45, 79, 83, 92, 113, 118, 119, 125, 164
Humbold-Klockner-Dautz, 50
Hurst Products, 32
Iacocca, Lee, 8, 10, 13–15, 18, 19, 21–23, 35, 32, 33, 39, 44, 45, 47, 55, 59, 63, 64, 85, 86, 116, 118, 139, 155, 157, 159, 162
Interior Decor Group, 47–49, 129
Johnson, Junior, 150
Joniec, Al, 110, 119
Kar Kraft Engineering, 20, 141, 143, 146, 149–152
Knudsen, Semon E. "Bunkie," 54, 55, 61–64, 66, 116, 119, 139, 140, 149, 152, 155, 159
Kopec, Rick, 97
Landy, Dick, 57
Larson Ford, 58
Lawton, Bill, 56, 57, 112
Lenox, Hank, 143
LIFE, 27, 32, 33, 97
Limited Production Option (LPO), 77
London Daily Herald, 21
Look, 27, 32
Lunn, Roy, 20, 25, 143, 151
Magaldi, Bud, 165
Maguire, Bob, 19
Matchbox, 32
Max Factor, 32
McCain, Don, 96
McLaughlin, Mathew, 62
McNamara, Robert, 18
Mel Burns Ford, 97
Mercury Cougar, 22, 25, 64, 69
Miles, Ken, 92
Miller, Arjay, 22
Misch, Herb, 19, 20
Mitchell, Bill, 24, 140
Moody, Ralph, 57
Morris, Tom, 135
Motor Trend, 13, 14, 21, 25, 64, 75, 88, 99, 134, 155, 160, 162
Murphy, Walt, 18
Mustang Indy 500 pacer pedal car, 32, 33
Mustang Models
    1962 Mustang I, 17–19
    1964 Indianapolis 500 pace car, 42, 43
    1964 Mustang II, 23
    1964, 27
    1964-1/2 convertible, 9, 27
    1964-1/2 coupe, 28
    1964-1/2, 29, 30, 38
    1965 2+2 fastback, 37
    1965 2+2 Tasca 505, 116
    1965 GT 350, 86, 89
    1965 GT 350R, 92

1965 GT, 70, 71, 74
1965, 29, 30
1965, 49
1966 GT 350, 92, 94, 99
1966 GT, 69, 74, 75
1967 390 GT, 82
1967 GT, 73, 75, 77, 78
1967 GTA convertible, 12
1967 GTA fastback, 77
1967 GTA, 73
1967 Shelby, 102, 104
1967 T-5 convertible, 50
1967, 47, 157
1968 390 GT, 82
1968 428 CJ, 143
1968 Cobra concept, 107
1968 Cobra Jet convertible, 112
1968 Cobra Jet, 110
1968 GT 500 Shelby, 118
1968 GT 500, 105
1968 GT 500KR, 104
1968 GT, 79, 82, 109
1968 KR-8, 113
1968, 52, 61
1968-1/2 CJ fastback, 113
1968-1/2 CJ, 118, 121
1968-1/2 Cobra Jet, 111, 115
1969 428 Cobra Jet Mach 1, 121
1969 Boss 302, 59, 60, 69, 127, 129, 139, 143, 148
1969 Boss 429, 59, 60, 69, 127, 146, 151
1969 GT 350, 100
1969 GT 350/500, 107
1969 GT 500, 102
1969 GT, 80
1969 Mach 1 SportsRoof, 127
1969 Mach 1, 59, 69, 127–129, 149
1970 Boss 302, 129, 139, 140, 148, 149
1970 Boss 351, 153, 154
1970 Boss 429, 147
1970 Boss 429, 152
1970 Grande, 59
1970 Mach 1, 130
1970 Shelby Mustang, 105
1970, 152
1971 Boss 351, 133, 134, 152, 155
1971 Cobra Jet Mach 1, 134
1971 coupe, 123
1971 Mach 1, 131–133
1971 Sports hardtop, 131, 133
1971, 61, 62, 66
1972 Mach 1, 134, 135, 137
1972 Olympic Sprint convertible, 63
1973 convertible, 66, 67
1973 Mach I, 137
1973, 67
1974 Mustang II, 15, 157, 159, 160
1976 Cobra II, 161
1978 King Cobra, 161
1978 Mustang II, 158
1979 Indianapolis 500 pace car, 159
1979 Indianapolis 500 pace car, 162
1979, 161, 162
1982 GT, 162

1983 GT, 164
1984 SVO, 161, 164
1984-1/2 20th Anniversary model, 160, 164
1988 5.0L LX, 164
1989 GT convertible, 162
1993 Cobra R, 167
1994 GT droptop, 9
1994 SVT Cobra coupe, 163
1994, 165
1995 Cobra R, 167
1999, 157, 166, 167
2+2 fastback, 41
2+2, 38
2000 Cobra R, 167
390 GT, 78
427 GT 500, 96, 97
427 Shelby, 97
427 Thunderbolt, 112
428 Cobra Jet, 139
429 Cobra Jet, 125
A/FX factory drag car, 56–58, 117
Boss 302, 55, 64, 140, 141, 143, 146
Boss 351, 123
Boss 429, 20, 55, 107, 141, 143, 145, 148, 149
Boss, 83
California Special, 55
CJ, 119, 121
Cobra Jet, 113
Grande, 66
GT 350 convertible, 99
GT 350 R, 91
GT 350 Shelby De Mexico, 103
GT 350, 85, 88, 91, 93, 94, 99, 102
GT 350H, 99
GT 350R, 86, 92
GT 500, 94, 104, 106, 114
GT 500KR, 99, 106
GT, 64, 69, 72, 82, 83, 128, 137
GT350H, 93
GT-40 Mk III, 116
GT-40, 20
Mach 1, 83
Mustang 2+2, 94
Mustang I, 21, 22, 25, 69
Mustang II, 24, 25, 51, 137
Olympic Sprint, 66
Shelby Cobra GT 350, 104
Shelby Cobra GT 500, 104
Shelby Mustang, 100, 106, 107
SportsRoof, 66, 137
T-5, 25, 50, 51
Mustang Monthly, 140
Mystery 9, 117
Najjar, John, 19, 21
National Advisory Committee for Aeronautics (NACA), 106, 124
National Aeronautics and Space Administration (NASA), 124
National Hot Rod Association (NHRA), 56
Naughton, John, 107
Newsweek, 8, 27, 42
Nicholson, Don "Dyno," 110, 119
O'Connor, Jim, 158, 167
Oros, Joe, 15, 22

Passino, Jacque, 18, 63
Petersen Publishing, 32
Petersen, Donald, 116
Peterson, Donald, 15, 18
Petty, Richard, 150
Platt, Hubert, 110, 119
Playboy, 32
Plymouth Barracuda, 10, 11, 64, 69
Plymouth Formula S Barracuda, 79
Plymouth Valiant, 17
Pontiac Firebird, 11, 54, 65, 69
Pontiac GTO, 32, 54
Pontiac Ram Air 400 Firebird, 79
Pontiac Trans Am Firebird, 64
Pontiac Trans Am, 65
Popular Hot Rodding, 136
Popular Science, 32
Rally-Pac option, 49, 75
Raviolo, Vic, 65
Rectrans, Inc., 152
Revson, Peter, 150
Rickmann, Eric, 92
Road & Track, 39, 71–73, 78, 92, 16
Ronda, Gas, 56, 58, 110
Ronny and the Daytonas, 32
Ronzi, Dick, 149
Rybicki, Irv, 64
Sanders, Bill, 134
Schmidt, Ken, 33
Shelby American, 85, 88, 89, 91, 92, 97, 104
Shelby, Carroll, 86, 88, 89, 92, 94, 9 99, 107, 114, 140, 167
Shinoda, Larry, 140, 141, 146, 152
Sipple, Jim, 19
Special Handling Package, 70, 71
Sperlich, Hal, 15, 18
Sports Car Graphic, 125, 129, 134, 1
Sports Cars of the World, 86
Sports Illustrated, 27, 32
SportsRoof, 59–61, 128, 132, 133, 150, 155
Stewart, Jackie, 43
Super Stock & Drag Illustrated, 125
Super Stock, 113, 116
Tasca Ford, 56, 97, 112, 113, 116, 1
Tasca, Bob Jr., 117
Tasca, Carl, 117
Tasca, David, 117
Tasca, Robert F. Jr., 112–114, 116–1
Telnack, Jack, 162
Thom McAn, 32
Time, 8, 27, 42
TomyToys, 32
Tucker, Captain Stanley, 34, 45
Velasquez, Eduardo, 103
Voss, Cliff, 11
Wall Street Journal, 32
Walter Hoving, Tiffany & Company, 34
Wilkins, Patrick, 33
Woods, Damon, 19, 47
Yarbrough, LeeRoy, 150
Yates, Brock, 107
Young, Cy, 13
Yunick, Smokey, 150
Zevalkink, Mike, 164